MW00980324

DEFORESTATION *in* VIET NAM

RODOLPHE DE KONINCK

INTERNATIONAL DEVELOPMENT RESEARCH CENTRE

Published by the International Development Research Centre
PO Box 8500, Ottawa, ON, Canada K1G 3H9

© International Development Research Centre 1999

Legal deposit: 1st quarter 1999
National Library of Canada
ISBN 0-88936-869-4

The views expressed are those of the author and do not necessarily represent those of the International Development Research Centre. Mention of a proprietary name does not constitute endorsement of the product and is given only for information. A microfiche edition is available.

The catalogue of IDRC Books may be consulted online at
http://www.idrc.ca/index_e.html

This book may be consulted online at http://www.idrc.ca/books/focus.html

CONTENTS

Foreword

Although the text that follows was written by a single person, namely, the undersigned, the research work on which it is based was carried out by a team of some 30 Vietnamese and Canadian researchers. This team was put together in 1992 and 1993, following a number of meetings that were made possible thanks to the support of the International Development Research Centre (IDRC). Christine Veilleux and I were heavily involved in this preliminary phase, following which a formal research proposal was submitted to IDRC. Once this proposal was approved, the actual project began, in April 1994. It was completed at the end of 1996, the last months being essentially devoted to the drafting of the final report. Comprising two volumes, this report was submitted in December 1996. Written in French, it was later redrafted in a shorter form and published by IDRC in October 1997 under the title *Le recul de la forêt au Viet Nam*. The present book is a translation, by its own author, of the original French version.

Entitled The Forest Challenge in Viet Nam, the research project pursued not only scientific goals (the identification, measurement, analysis, and interpretation of the causes of deforestation) but also an educational goal (the training of young Vietnamese and Canadian researchers). Furthermore, reliance on cartographic representation and analysis was built into the project design, with the Canadian participants finding it among their mandates to share their cartographic knowledge and skills with their Vietnamese counterparts. The fieldwork (whether involving the direct observation of deforestation processes and related phenomena or the collection of various types of data) and the processing of that material, particularly for the purpose of synthesizing it in the form of maps, involved a large number of people.

The participants who contributed directly to the actual research came from Laval University, primarily from its Geography Department, and from several Vietnamese institutions: the Centre for Natural Resources and Environmental Studies (CRES), attached to the National University of Vietnam (at one time known as the University of Hanoi); the Human Geography Research Centre, itself attached to the National Centre for Social Sciences and also based in Hanoi; the Forest Inventory and Planning Institute, whose offices are located a few kilometres south of Hanoi; and, finally, the University of Agriculture and Forestry (UAF) (now called the College of Agriculture and Forestry), located in Thu Duc, south of Ho Chi Minh City. The two Vietnamese research directors were Professor Vo Quy and Professor Luu Trong Hieu, attached to CRES and UAF, respectively.

The main Vietnamese researchers from the northern institutions were Vo Thanh Son, Dao Minh Truong, Duong Tri Hung, Nguyen Hong Quang, Pham Hong Quang, Dang Duc Phuong, Lam Thi Mai Lan, Bui Quang Toan, Nguyen Ngoc Toan, and Dang Huy Huynh; and from the southern institutions, Tran Dac Dan, Hoang Huu Cai, Nguyen Duc Binh, Vo Van Thoan, Lam Xuan Sanh, Le Xuan Canh, Nguyen Minh Duong, Nguyen Thuc Huyen, Nguyen Ngoc Thuy, Pham Dinh Hung, and Nguyen Van Dieu.

Besides the undersigned, the Laval University team comprised Stéphane Bernard, François Brassard (whose work was supervised by Professor Pierre Bellefleur), Steve Déry, Lyne Chabot, Olivier Lundqvist, Luisa Molina, Youssouph Sane, Christine Veilleux, and Yann Roche. The latter and Olivier Lundqvist handled the crucial and very demanding responsibility of coordinating and finalizing all the cartographic work. Several of the project's Vietnamese participants were also very instrumental in the preparation of the maps, notably, Vo Thanh Son, Tran Dac Dan, Hoang Huu Cai, Nguyen Duc Binh, and Vo Van Thoan. The maps illustrating this English version of the book were prepared by Olivier Lundqvist and Stéphane Bernard.

Quite a few other persons were involved in one way or another in this venture. This group comprised several Vietnamese scholars and civil servants, but it would be inappropriate to list them all here. I do wish, however, to single out and emphasize the importance of the unfailing and efficient support provided by Stephen Tyler, a senior program officer at IDRC, and Jingjai Hanchanlash, program manager of the Vietnam Sustainable and Economic Development project. The project also benefited from the advice of Terry Rambo, whose excellent work in Viet Nam converged with this research, especially with regard to the conclusions concerning the uplands of the country and their indigenous inhabitants.

Most of the funds for this project were provided by IDRC, but related research endeavours, carried out in Viet Nam and in several other Southeast Asian countries, were backed by the Social Sciences and Humanities Research Council of Canada and by the Fonds international de coopération universitaire program of the Association des universités partiellement et entièrement de langue française.

To all the above mentioned institutions and persons, I wish to express my gratitude and offer my sincere thanks.

Rodolphe De Koninck
Department of Geography
Laval University
Québec, April 1998

Chapter 1

INTRODUCTION: THE NATURE AND MAGNITUDE OF THE PROBLEM

Between the late 1960s and the late 1990s, Southeast Asia's forest cover was reduced from 66% to 49% of the region's total land area (Figures 1 and 2; Table 1). It can be estimated that by 2000, the forests' overall extent will have dropped well below 40%, perhaps as low as 33%. In practically every country of the region, in coastal and lowland areas as well as in the highlands, forests continue to lose ground at such a pace that the overall environmental equilibrium is threatened. In addition, it seems evident that although all forest types are submitted to the onslaught, two are being taken to task with particular intensity: the mountain rain forests, which are the richest in terms of biomass and biodiversity; and the mangrove forests, which are narrow coastal amphibious formations, already very limited in extent and one of the most vulnerable types of rain forests.

The problem is ominous for at least three major reasons, quite distinct from one another. The first two pertain to the nature and the very contents of tropical forests, whereas the third is related to the history of world development.

An exceptional biodiversity

The flora of tropical forests, particularly that of rain forests, is exceptionally diverse. On average, 1 ha contains — besides a large number of plants, ferns, and flowers — 50–200 species of trees, whereas temperate forests rarely contain more than 10 (Collins 1990). All by themselves, tropical forests hold more than two-thirds of the 250 000 superior plants known to scientists (Whitmore 1990). In fact, the inventory of tropical flora — as well as of the fauna that thrive on this flora, including some 30 million species of insects — is far from complete and never will be, considering the actual rates of deforestation in the tropical world (Collins 1990).

Biodiversity, or richness in floral or faunal species, appears that much more remarkable given that it is characterized by endemism. It is not rare, for example, for a majority of tree and butterfly species growing and living in a given

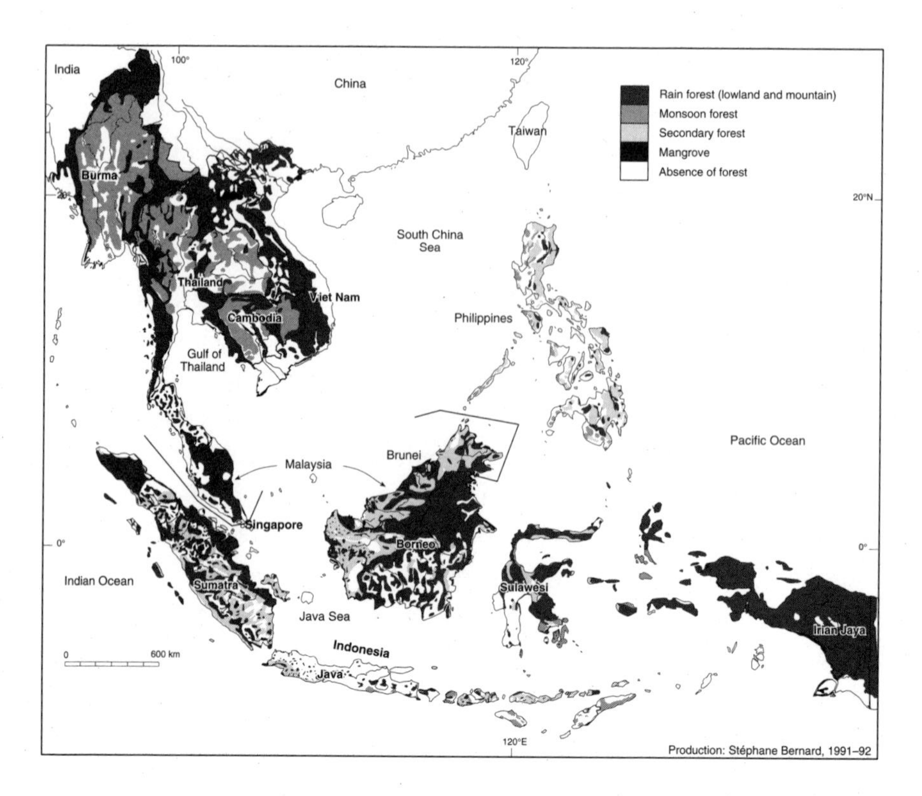

Figure 1. Southeast Asia's forest cover, circa 1970. Source: IGA (1969); Weltforstat Atlas (1971); Whitmore (1984); Collins (1990); Collins et al. (1991); Bernard and De Koninck (1996).

forest sector and covering but a few hectares to exist nowhere else. This characteristic, common to all rain forests, has major implications for the way the planet's genetic heritage — whether floral or faunal — must be managed, particularly in view of its enormous value as an actual or potential source of food and medicine.

Plants and animals depend on each other, not only for nutrition, but also for reproduction. All animals — whether insects, birds, bats, or even fish in the swamps and amphibian forests — unconsciously act as disseminators of seeds and pollen when they move about. Multiple and complex, the symbioses between certain species are sometimes specific to such a degree that the disappearance of one of them may bring about a disastrous chain reaction.

All tropical rain forests generate an enormous quantity of vegetation, as much as 25–30 t/ha of new growth per annum. This is twice as much as an oak forest generates and three times as much as a boreal coniferous forest generates

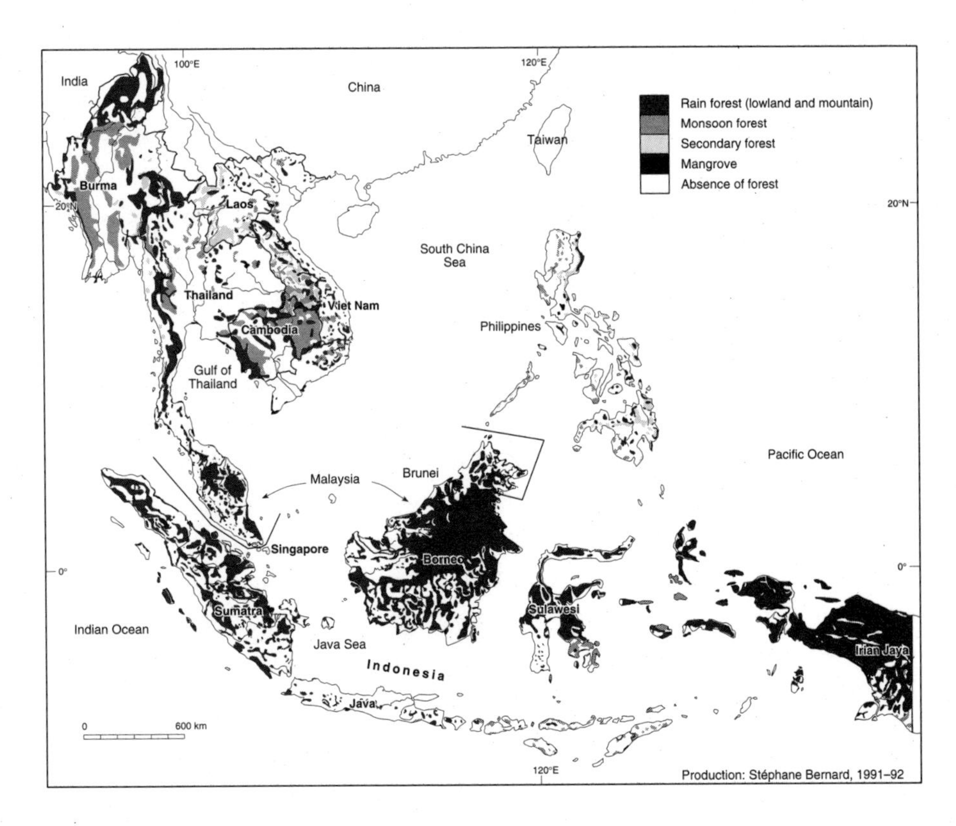

Figure 2. Southeast Asia's forest cover, circa 1990. Source: Collins (1990); Collins et al. (1991); Bernard and De Koninck (1996).

Table 1. Southeast Asia: area and changes in forest cover, late 1960s to late 1980s.

Main countries	Total area (km^2)	Area covered with forest: Late 1960s (km^2)	Late 1960s (%)	Late 1980s (km^2)	Late 1980s (%)
Cambodia	181 000	135 750	75	113 250	63
Indonesia	913 000	1 422 909	74	1 179 140	62
Laos	237 000	165 900	70	124 600	53
Malaysia	330 000	273 047	83	200 420	61
Myanmar	677 000	440 050	65	311 850	46
Philippines	300 000	150 000	50	66 020	22
Thailand	513 000	256 500	50	149 600	24
Viet Nam	330 000	181 500	55	56 680	17

Source: IGA (1969); Weltforstat Atlas (1971); Whitmore (1984); Collins (1990); Collins et al. (1991).

(Collins 1990). Often growing on poor soils, the tropical rain forests draw an exceptionally large proportion of their requirements from solar energy and the heavy rainfall and the rest from the results of the decomposition of the abundant biomass. The work of decomposers, such as bacteria and fungi, generates nutritional elements, such as nitrogen, phosphorous, and iron, that are indispensable to plants and animals. In such forests, the total per hectare biomass may reach 500 t, a performance that is again largely superior to that of temperate forests.

Rich but also vulnerable and inhabited forests

Rain forests are not only qualitatively different from forests that used to grow or are still growing under temperate climates but also much more vulnerable and threatened, although the world's ecological future depends on their survival.

This enormous genetic store plays an essential role in the water and carbon cycles. Although the actual nature and importance of this role are still the subject of debate, it is generally accepted that the retreat of the tropical rain forests is having an impact on rainfall patterns. Through transpiration and evaporation, these forests return to the atmosphere half to three-quarters of the moisture they receive from rains, and these rains are, on average, much more abundant than those that fall in most temperate regions. Once a rain forest has been cleared off the land, the amount of moisture rapidly made available to the rain cycle is considerably reduced. In addition, surface runoff is greatly accelerated, with frequently catastrophic consequences.

In fact, the ecological vulnerability of tropical rain forests is in part due to the fact that once the land is denuded, even if only partially, the soil is very prone to erosion. This in turn is also partly linked to a characteristic of the large rain-forest trees, which tend to have a less developed underground root system. In addition, the forest formations to which they belong are increasingly confined to mountainous areas. Where the forest cover is markedly depleted, the strong equatorial rainfall easily and rapidly erodes away the topsoil, with the frequent result that areas once rich in plant and animal life have become arid and at times barely adequate for cultivation. Nothing so efficiently reduces the impact of heavy downpours as the thick tropical moist forest.

Finally, tropical rain forests are still largely inhabited, much more so than temperate forests, which are much poorer in floral and faunal resources, ever were. Although temperate forests are also occupied and used by human communities, they have less frequently been relied on as places of exclusive residence. Tropical rain forests have been inhabited for some 39 000 years in Borneo and 12 000 years in the Amazon Basin. In fact, it is estimated that throughout the entire tropical world, nearly 50 million people live within their realm (Collins 1990); about half of these live in Southeast Asia. Forest people are first and foremost tropical-forest people. Such forest dwellers, particularly the hunter–gatherers, but also the shifting cultivators, are the legatees of irreplaceable knowledge, especially concerning forest biodiversity, its uses, and the ways to protect and maintain it. Unfortunately, these forest dwellers are themselves everywhere endangered, either by the expansion of commercial logging or by the advance of agricultural pioneers, who more often than not follow in the footsteps of the loggers (Colchester 1993).

Although in most of the countries concerned, management policies, both for protection and for replanting, have been adopted, their implementation remains problematic and haphazard, if only because the actual mechanisms behind forest depletion and, particularly, their articulations are insufficiently identified and hence ill-understood.

The scramble toward growth and development

Notwithstanding recent slowdowns, the contemporary pace of economic growth of Southeast Asian nations is far superior to that experienced by the now industrial countries, particularly those of Europe. Given also the superior population-growth ratios and the resulting much higher population densities, the pressure exerted on the resources of Southeast Asia is that much more significant.

From the 16th century on, the expansion of the European economies was partly achieved at the expense of non-European territories or, at least, thanks to their resources and the provision of their own lands for European settlement. This resulted in a proportionate reduction, during given periods, of the pressure on natural resources and on the overall environment of several of the countries now fully industrialized.[1] Southeast Asian countries have no access to such relief for their forests, or when they do, it is not nearly so significant.

The world economic system, basically devised by the industrial nations and their multinational corporations, requires tropical wood, together with a certain number of the products of plantation agriculture. This being said, it must be remembered that the major providers of forest products on the world market are by far Canada, Russian Federation, and the United States. In fact, most industrial countries have been managing and protecting their forests with improving efficiency, with the result that their own forest-cover ratios have increased over the

[1]This argument is often ignored by economic historians who, like Bairoch (1995), argue on the sole basis of econometric measures that the now industrialized world did not draw any real economic benefit from its colonial empires.

last decades, if not centuries. In France, for example, the turnaround began in the late 19th century; in the United States, in the very early 20th century; and in Japan, in the 1950s, at a time when the retreat of Southeast Asian forests was about to undergo considerable acceleration (De Koninck 1998).

Chapter 2
THE CASE OF VIET NAM

The specificity of Viet Nam's case

A lowland civilization

"The rich and beautiful forests of Vietnam have always been prominent in the history and culture of the Vietnamese people" (Sargent 1991, p. 3). Unfortunately, such a claim, though frequently found in Vietnamese publications, does not really correspond to reality, that is, if by Vietnamese culture is meant the culture of the Kinh or Viet people. Although forests have indeed occupied a prominent place in the cultural world of Viet Nam's minority peoples, most of whom were historically confined to the mountainous and forested regions of the country's interior, such has not been the case with the Kinh. In fact, until recently, the vast majority of the latter chose to settle in the coastal and deltaic regions of the country. As with most dominant peoples around which the modern states of Southeast Asia were formed, the Viet are a lowland people, specializing in wet rice cultivation. Along with several such peoples — the Javanese, for example — the Kinh have essentially stayed away from forested areas and have systematically avoided settling in them. Forests have remained the realm of minority peoples, who have predominantly chosen to practice slash-and-burn cultivation, whether or not it involves shifting their places of residence.

Only fairly recently, during the 1920s, under the French colonial administration, did planned-colonization programs contribute, with very limited success however, to the expansion of Kinh settlement toward the Central Highlands (also known as the Central Plateaus). These programs were associated with attempts to sedentarize the highland minorities (Hickey 1982a; Hill 1985), about which a negative discourse became prominent among the colonial administrators (Buchy 1993; Brocheux and Hémery 1994). During the 1930s, penetration of the forested highlands became a clearly strategic matter, as the Vietnamese revolutionary forces used this area as both a hideaway and a tactical launching pad in wars against the French and, later on, the Americans. In addition, during the Ngo Dinh Diem regime's administration of South Viet Nam (1955–63), large contingents of refugees from the North, mostly Catholics, were settled in the Central Highlands. Finally and more importantly, modern forms of agricultural expansion, particularly since the 1975/76 reunification, have consolidated and amplified the agrarian conquest of a realm long considered marginal, even taboo.

Equivalent or at least comparable processes have been active in several countries of the region, although the prevailing factors, rhythms, and contingencies involved may differ. Nevertheless, just about everywhere, the expansion of the central settlements proceeds from the lowlands and moves in the direction of the mountainous peripheral areas, which are generally forested and are inhabited by minority peoples (De Koninck and Déry 1997).

A considerable ecological differentiation

One of Viet Nam's major geographical characteristics is its elongated shape: its narrow territory spreads more than 2 000 km from north to south, between latitudes 8° and 23°N. Essentially located within the tropics, the country also has an exceptionally long coastal development, extending more than about 5 230 km (Morgan and Valencia 1983). In addition, notwithstanding the two large deltas of the Red River (Song Hong) and the Mekong River and the narrow coastal plains that link them, the country is predominantly mountainous: hills, plateaus, and mountains occupy nearly three-quarters of the land. The combination of these characteristics — that is, an extended and coastal tropicality and an exceptionally hilly interior — is favourable to biodiversity. This pertains to not only the various types of inland rain forests but also the mangrove forests — situated along the country's coasts, particularly those of the Mekong Delta — as well as the large pine forests of the Central Highlands.

Recently, Vo Quy and Le Thac Can (1994, p. 56) referred to the presence in Viet Nam of some

> 12,000 species of higher vascular plants, of which more than 7,000 have been identified ..., 800 species of mosses and 600 species of mushrooms ..., 276 of mammals, 820 of birds, 180 of reptiles, 80 of amphibians, 472 of freshwater fish.

A seriously threatened forest heritage

Unfortunately, over the last 50 years or so, this remarkable Vietnamese forest heritage has been gravely undermined. According to the most frequently quoted sources, between 1943 and 1993 the proportion of the national territory covered by forests declined from at least 43% to 20% (Vo Quy 1996) or even to as low as 16% (Table 2) — the various estimates differ somewhat, depending on the authors and their respective sources. Some observers go as far as claiming that the proportion of Viet Nam still covered by forests has now fallen below 10%.

This impressive retreat of the forest has been accompanied by an equally disturbing process, also active in other countries in the region, notably the Philippines and Indonesia: the rapid spread of denuded or barren lands. Although a substantial proportion of forest-covered lands gives way to permanent agriculture, another proportion, at least equally extensive, is left barren. This is generally the result of a few years of excessive cropping, followed by the land's being abandoned and left prey to erosion, with the result that rapid leaching of the topsoil occurs and the land becomes literally barren. Apparently, by the early 1990s, as much as 40% of Viet Nam's land was in such a state (Vo Quy et Le Thac Can 1994).

Notwithstanding the obvious need to measure as accurately as possible the relative impact of each of the factors and general conditions involved in these changes in the forest cover, it is at least possible at this stage to list the most obvious ones:

- The wars, particularly those that devastated the country between 1945 and 1975;
- A very high rate of population growth, until recently well above 2% per annum;
- An already very high population density, about 235 inhabitants/km^2 (at the end of 1997, some 77 millions inhabitants on 330 000 km^2), the highest in Southeast Asia (leaving aside Singapore);

Table 2. Viet Nam: changes in forest cover, 1943–96.

	Proportion of Viet Nam covered with forest (%)						
Source	1943	1973	1975	1982	1983	1987	1993
MOF (1991)	43.0	29.0	—	—	—	28.0	—
Do Dinh Sam (1994)	40.7	—	28.6	—	23.6	—	27.7
Vo Quy and Le Thac Can (1994)	~46.0	—	—	—	—	—	—
Le Thac Can and Vo Quy (1994)	<44.0	—	—	23.0	24.0	—	—
Vo Quy (1996)	43.0	—	—	—	—	—	—
WCMC (1996)	—	—	—	—	—	—	16.0

- Widespread inefficiency in the management of resources, related to, among other things, a frequent lack of coordination between the various levels of governments;

- Prevailing national policies of economic growth at all costs; and

- Excessive reliance on forest resources, notably for energy production, in a country endowed with insufficient, inadequate, and overtaxed infrastructure.

However, the mere reference to all these factors, to all these macroeconomic and macrogeographic conditions, is insufficient without the identification of their articulations and of the very processes of deforestation.

In addition, in Viet Nam, researchers make no attempt to deconstruct the processes and mechanisms that lead to deforestation; rather, the tendency is to simply refer to the various reforestation programs, presumably under the pretext that these programs are likely to compensate for the current forest retreat. Unfortunately, for a number of reasons, the success of these programs remains limited. For example, in terms of area covered, the rate of reforestation remains well below that of deforestation;[2] and replanted forests, including those that supply the pulp and paper industry, have a very low survival rate and are in terms of biomass and biodiversity far less productive than the natural forests.

In other words, the retreat of the forests will continue as long as the real causes and the actual agents and processes of deforestation are not clearly identified, their articulations are not fully understood, and the causes are not at least brought under control, if not eliminated. In short, Viet Nam must find the means to take up and counter the forest challenge. Time is running out. If comprehensive policies (assuming that the political will to devise and implement them does exist in the country) and efficient policies of management, protection, and reconstitution of the forest cover are not implemented at a broad national scale, Viet Nam may soon have to cope with a major deterioration of its natural environment, with catastrophic social and economic consequences.

[2] According to Vo Quy and Le Thac Can (1994), by the mid-1990s, the annual replanting rate reached 100 000–160 000 ha, against 200 000 ha being deforested. It must be remembered that most replanting programs have so far relied on single-species plantings and in several cases on ill-adapted species of the eucalyptus type. Whatever the case, given that the proportion of the national territory currently covered by forest is 10–20% (that is, 3.3–6 million ha), the annual rate of depletion of natural forest cover must be between 6% and 3%.

Ambiguous interpretations

The responsibility of the ethnic minorities?

Of course, interpretations of the causes of deforestation in Viet Nam, as well as in other countries of Southeast Asia, are not in short supply. Here, as elsewhere, the finger is pointed at high population-growth ratios and the resulting increased demographic pressure, overall development needs, energy requirements, agricultural imperatives — and ethnic minorities. In fact, many claim that these people, with their slash-and-burn or swidden cultivation, are still largely responsible for the retreat of the forest. Yet, in Viet Nam, as elsewhere, these claims are insufficiently documented, as they are often based on unsubstantiated generalizations. Although they have often been refuted — for example, by Condominas (1957), Dove (1983), and Boulbet (1975, 1995) — these allegations are still frequently made.[3]

In Viet Nam, such allegations were particularly widespread at the time of the French colonial administration, with geographers, ethnographers, and foresters all claiming that the ethnic minorities had a primitive and destructive way of life (for example, Gourou 1940). Similar allegations were recently taken up again by a Vietnamese ethnologist, who stated that ethnic minorities were responsible for as much as 25% of the estimated 200 000 ha of annual deforestation occurring in Viet Nam (Nguyen Van Thang 1995). In no way substantiated, this statement is still more moderate than those proffered by many Vietnamese civil servants as well as by equally numerous international advisers, who attribute to the ethnic minorities as much as half of the deforestation, always without serious proof. In fact, Nguyen Van Thang, who claimed that ethnic minorities are responsible for 25% of the destruction of Viet Nam's forests, attributed the rest of the destruction, the whole three-quarters of it, to agricultural expansion. He did this without any explanation or any consideration of other plausible causes, such as the development of transport infrastructure, commercial logging — whether legal or illegal — and local populations' nibbling at the forest to obtain wood for a number of purposes, including fuel.[4]

---

[3]For a recent and well-documented debunking of these allegations, see Thrupp et al. (1997).

[4]One must recognize, however, that other observers of the Vietnamese scene are more discerning, such as Do Dinh Sam, who recently published a solid study of itinerant agriculture in Viet Nam. According to Do Dinh Sam (1994), as many as 50 of the 54 ethnic minorities practice some form of shifting cultivation; these communities comprise some 3 million people. See also Sargent (1991), as well as Rambo (1995), who recently reiterated that itinerant agriculture is not in itself destructive.

The destruction of war?

The wars that raged on and off for nearly 50 years throughout Viet Nam are among the factors in deforestation. But the long-lasting evaluation of their impact remains ambiguous and contradictory. Thus, not long ago, Collins (1990, p. 158) went as far as to write that "from 1945 to 1975, almost uninterrupted warfare resulted in the destruction of most of the remaining forest and farmland, giving rise to a new word — *ecocide*."[5] Yet, in the same book, one page farther on (Collins 1990, p. 159), one can read that "American and Vietnamese scientists estimate that 22,000 square kilometers of forest and one-fifth of the country's farmland were affected as a direct result of bombing, mechanized land clearing and defoliation." Is it necessary for us to point out that 22 000 km^2 (or 2.2 million ha) is equal to 6.6% of Viet Nam's total surface area and to 15.6% of the area covered by forests in 1943 and 23% in 1973 (according to the figures quoted in the *Vietnam Forestry Sector Review* [MOF 1991]; see also Table 1)? That's quite different from Collins' "most of the remaining forest."

Other factors?

Besides the exaggerated statements concerning the consequences of both the slash-and-burn cultivation practiced by the ethnic minorities and the wars, particularly the American war, another overstatement is common. This one concerns the agricultural potential of Viet Nam's Central Highlands. At the beginning of the early 1920s, these highlands were still almost entirely covered with forests and nearly exclusively inhabited by ethnic minorities. Since then they have been the object of several agricultural-colonization efforts on the part of the Kinh, with the first major ones having been sponsored by the French colonial administration. For strategic and economic purposes, the French colonials aimed at further integrating the highlands and its inhabitants into their overall Indochinese domain, both by attempting to sedentarize these inhabitants and by encouraging the inmigration of Kinh peasants.[6] Various postcolonial administrations pursued such attempts at colonizing the highlands, including the Diem administration in South Viet Nam (1955–63). But the systematic penetration of the Central Plateaus was only really

---

[5]On the concept of ecocide, see Weisberg (1970).

[6]Several authors have either described or interpreted these policies, including Maurand (1943, 1968), Hickey (1982a, b), Hill (1985), Buchy (1993), Pouchepadass (1993), and Brocheux and Hémery (1994). Few, if any, seem to have understood that this practice of sedentarizing nomads and of moving lowland peasants to the margins of the central Vietnamese domain was simply a local version of a long-established and nearly universal strategy. That strategy consists in a state's using the small landed peasantry as both its territorial spearhead and the custodian of its territorial legitimacy (De Koninck 1986, 1993, 1996).

launched following the 1975/76 reunification, with the massive development of the New Economic Zones (NEZs). Since then the highlands have become frontier land, with the ever-advancing pioneer fronts often leaving large tracts of barren land in their wake, where any regrowth of vegetation appears highly problematic. Nevertheless, some observers still claim that in the Central Plateaus vast expanses of fertile land, notably the famed basaltic soils, are still available for the expansion of agriculture (Tran Thi Van An and Nguyen Manh Huan 1995).

In total, notwithstanding the numerous and in many cases excellent studies dealing with the problem of deforestation in Viet Nam, none suggests, let alone contains, a systematic and rigorous analysis of the real causes of the retreat of the forests. Of course, interpretations of the role of one or two specific factors are frequent. But, to my knowledge, none of these interpretations results from attempts to empirically verify a set of hypotheses.

Observers, even decision-makers, frequently cite with fatalism the major causes. These are, as stated above, population growth, economic development, and the need for more agricultural land, more energy production, and more exports. But these observers rarely if ever refer to the mechanisms linking these causes, the instruments on which they rely, or their specific local impacts.

Chapter 3

THE IMPLEMENTATION OF THE RESEARCH PROJECT

The hypotheses

Fundamental and instrumental causes

The fundamental general causes of deforestation in Viet Nam are demographic growth; economic growth; an increasing demand for food and export crops; and an increasing demand for forest products — primarily wood for the pulp and paper industry, for construction, and for fuel. It should be understood that these types of demand are not tied exclusively to population growth, whether local or global. For example, it is quite evident that the expansion in the cultivation of rubber trees or of coffee and cashew trees cannot be attributed to a demand generated solely by the increase in the population of Viet Nam or of any other country. Agricultural expansion, essentially achieved at the expense of the forest domain, is the result of a decision-making process, which is itself based on the recognition of a number of economic, political, and geostrategic factors, some of which may be considered imperative, others contingent. But I add here that for these general causes to become operational, they must be articulated to instrumental causes. If all of these were clearly identified, Vietnamese authorities not only would be in a position to influence the general conditions and causes, but also would be more easily able to slow down, deflect, or even block the instrumental causes.

We were unable to accurately measure the actual extent of any given general cause. Nor do we yet know the exact impact of a specific instrumental factor of deforestation. We are, however, in a position to identify the more important among these instrumental factors and to regroup them into the following four main categories:

- An excessive practice of itinerant agriculture by some representatives of ethnic minorities;

- Agricultural expansion and what frequently comes along with it, namely, a reliance on slash-and-burn techniques, too often mistaken by many observers for a form of the above-mentioned itinerant agriculture;

- Logging, whether legal or illegal; and

- Collection of forest products for survival, including fruits and plants; wood, bamboo, and rattan to be used in the construction of dwellings and in the cottage industries; and, foremost, firewood.

Obviously, other factors have been at play: this is the case with war, as a fundamental cause, and with one of its major tools of forest destruction — defoliants.

It is equally evident that the four main contemporary instruments retained here are constantly interactive. For example, agricultural expansion is likely to exert considerable territorial pressure on traditional slash-and-burn cultivators to such an extent that they often shorten the fallow period for their swidden fields and end up cultivating more difficult terrain, such as steep slopes, with dire consequences, especially soil erosion. Agricultural expansion may also bring about an increase in predatory practices among the new settlers, who tend to rely excessively on the forests to meet their needs, particularly their energy needs. Such reliance on forest resources may, without any agricultural expansion being involved, emanate from stable, long-established communities' facing deterioration of their other sources of supplies, including that caused by unaffordability. In addition, the spatial extension of agriculture is often associated with the development of commercial logging; at times, the two progress simultaneously, and at times the one precedes the other, as when the opening of roads for the one facilitates the progress of the other.

The hypotheses: a central instrumental cause and its articulations

Consequently, it seems essential to identify the articulations that link together these various instrumental factors of deforestation. Better still, one should, ideally, identify and measure the direction, intensity, and even ranking of these articulations. This requires a search for the central instrument of deforestation, the prime destructor of forests.

We therefore formulate the following hypothesis: agricultural expansion is indeed the central instrument of deforestation in Viet Nam. Furthermore, this expansion would tend to play a crucial geopolitical role to the extent that it allows the central state both to consolidate its control over the margins of the national territory and to accelerate the integration of the ethnic minorities into the national social fabric. This double proposition leads to two additional ones. First, most of the other major instrumental factors are linked to agricultural expansion through a series of mechanisms that vary but remain identifiable. Second, some of these factors, including the pivotal one (agricultural expansion), are not necessarily imperative or unavoidable. On the contrary, they may be contingent: in other words, the Vietnamese authorities may be able to neutralize or block them. But, for that to happen, the factors must be properly identified. This brings us to our research project, which relied on a hypothetico-deductive approach.

The research methodology

The geographical scale of the study and its location

Ideally, our study should have covered the whole of Viet Nam, and for a while we did consider testing our hypotheses at the scale of the entire country. But our enthusiasm was quickly quenched by the difficulties we met in assembling the data necessary for the verification of our propositions, whether these data concerned historical or contemporary phenomena and processes.

To put our hypotheses to the test, it seemed to us essential to rely on diachronic measurements of both the changes in forest cover and the presumed fundamental and instrumental factors. Unfortunately, land-use data in Viet Nam turned out to be quite fragmentary, particularly those from the past. Moreover, all types of data — photos, maps, statistics, etc. — whether contemporary or historical, are in many cases unreliable. Historical documents are especially unreliable. All these data are either incomplete, particularly for reasons of war, or too contradictory and inadequate to be assessed and plotted on a spatial basis. Administrative divisions and boundaries — whether those of provinces, districts, or communes — have been modified several times over the past few decades; in fact the administrative map of Viet Nam is constantly being modified. Finally, the country is poor and is also under permanent administrative reorganization, with the often conflicting responsibilities and prerogatives of the various levels of government being frequently altered. As a consequence, various types of data that should be of a public nature become in reality the private property of a given public servant or groups of such servants; these data henceforth bear a price, at times quite substantial, particularly if they take the form of maps. And even if they carry a price, the data obtained from statutory institutions, including census-related ones, must be handled with caution, for they have at times been "adapted."

In view of such problems, it quickly became clear that we had to confine ourselves to measuring the retreat of the forest and its presumed factors at a more modest scale, namely, that of two provinces. The eventual choice of these two provinces, Tuyen Quang and Lam Dong, was based on several criteria: size; relative extent and importance of forests; presence of ethnic minorities; location (the first province is in the northern part of the country, and the second is in the southern part); accessibility; and feasibility, including the support of the local authorities (Figures 3a and 3b; Tables 3 and 4).

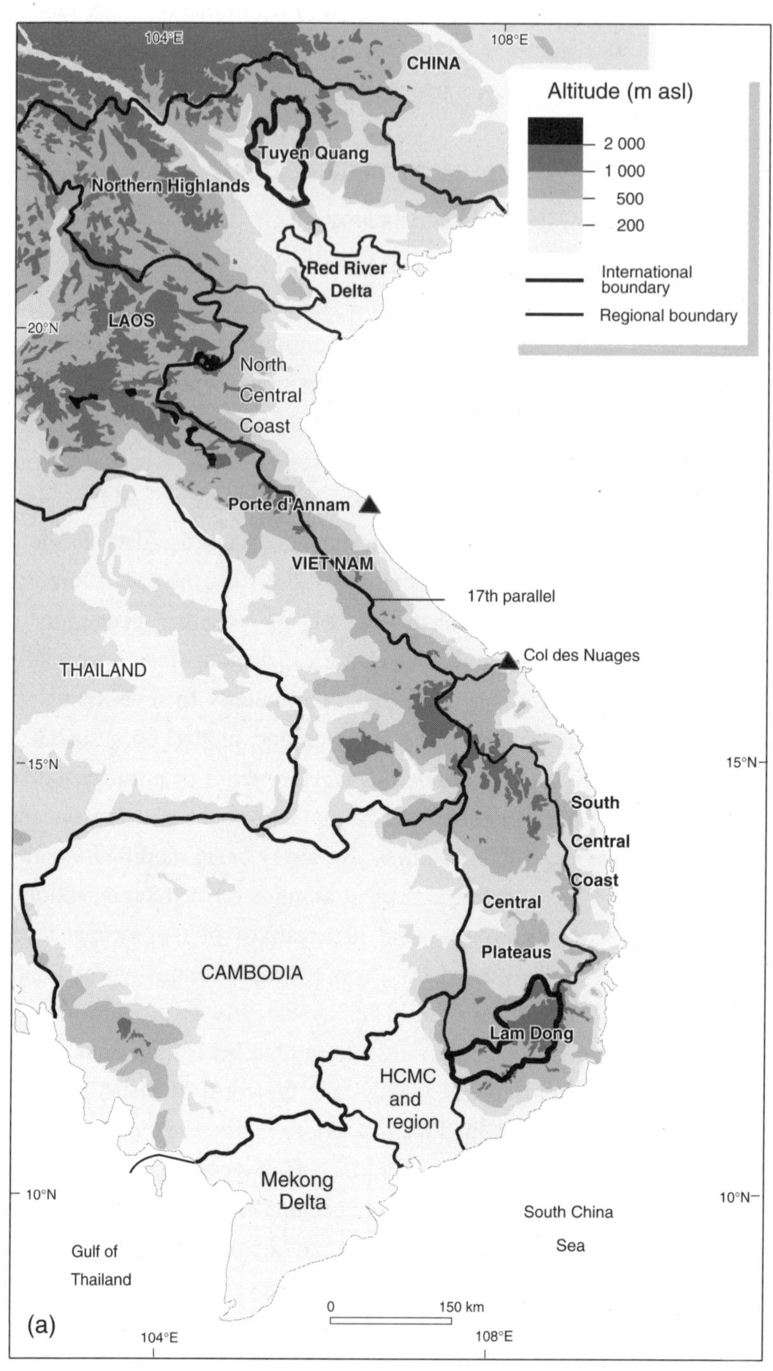

Figure 3a. Tuyen Quang and Lam Dong provinces in Viet Nam. Source: Lebar et al. (1964). Note: HCMC, Ho Chi Minh City; m asl, metres above sea level.

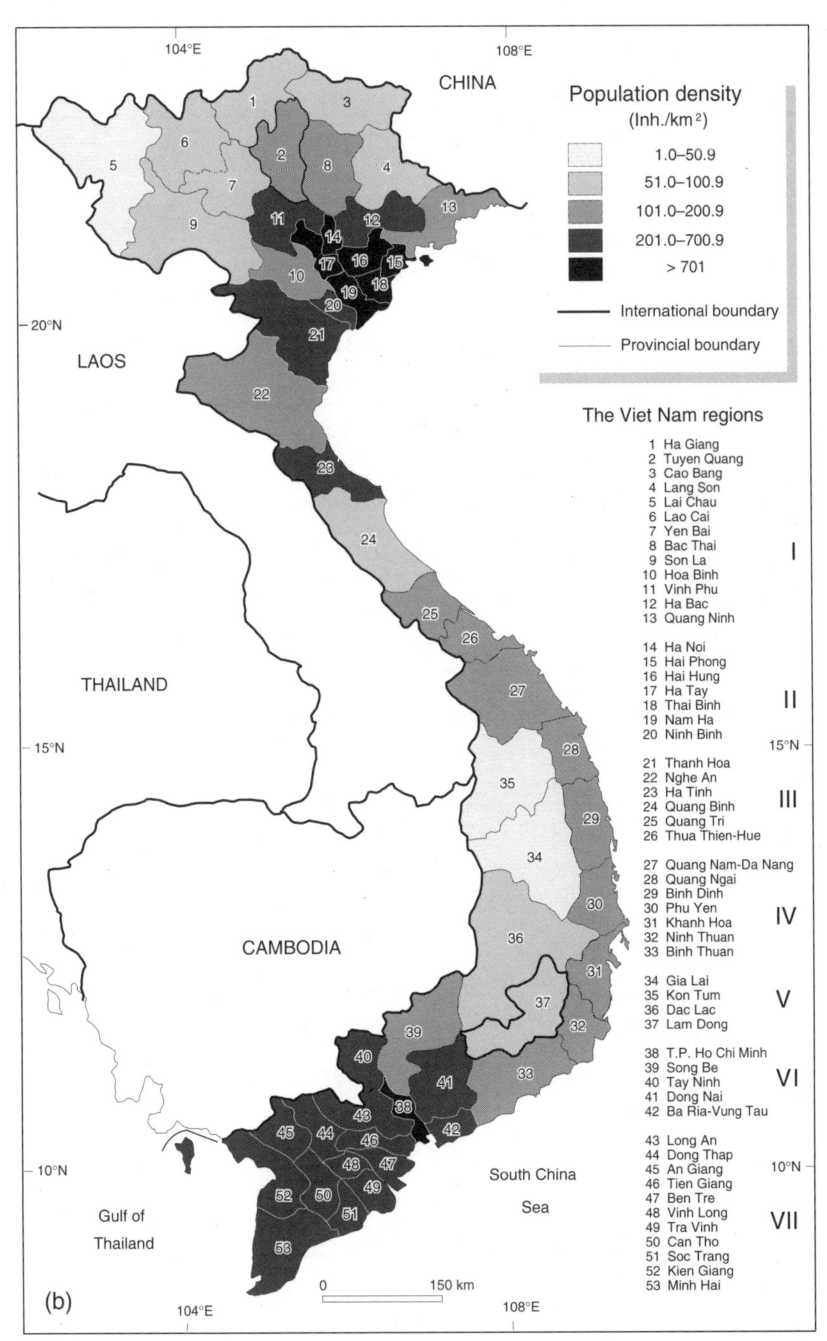

Figure 3b. Viet Nam: population density by province, 1991. Source: De Koninck (1994). Note: inh., inhabitants.

Table 3. Tuyen Quang province: area, population, and population density, by district, 1989 and 1992.

	Area (km^2)	Population		Population density (inhabitants/km^2)	
		1989	1992	1989	1992
Chiem Hoa	1 413	103 540	112 045	73	79
Ham Yen	938	1 857	89 136	87	95
Na Hang	1 470	50 944	56 140	35	38
Son Duong	810	140 366	154 247	173	190
Tuyen Quang [a]	43	47 482	52 542	1 104	1 221
Yen Son	1 231	140 334	153 305	114	126
Province	5 905	565 095	617 415	96	105

Source: The last Vietnamese census dates back to 1989. The data for 1992, provided by the Tuyen Quang Provincial Statistics Bureau, were in fact projections (about 109%), made more or less uniformly from the 1989 census.

Note: In 1976, Tuyen Quang province was regrouped with the former military region of Ha Giang to form Ha Tuyen province. In 1991, Ha Tuyen province was in turn broken up into two provinces, Ha Giang and Tuyen Quang. Of course, this immensely complicates the use of and reliance on historical statistics (see Figure 4).

[a] Municipality.

Table 4. Lam Dong province: area, population, and population density, by district, 1989.

	Area (km^2)	Population	Population density (inhabitants/km^2)
Bao Loc	1 773	128 587	73
Cat Tien	359	25 933	72
Da Hoai	573	22 040	38
Da Lat [a]	419	115 959	277
Da Teh	473	34 498	73
Di Linh	1 570	75 007	48
Don Duong	639	60 204	94
Duc Trong	897	99 552	111
Lac Duong	1 882	17 974	10
Lam Ha	1 588	59 470	37
Province	10 173	639 224	63

Source: National Census of Viet Nam.

Note: Lam Dong became a province even more recently than Tuyen Quang (see note to Table 3). In addition, since 1976 the boundaries of its districts and communes have been modified on numerous occasions (see Figures 4 and 15).

[a] Township.

The small town of Tuyen Quang, the capital of the province bearing the same name, is about 5 h by road from the national capital, Hanoi, or, more precisely, from the University of Hanoi (now called the National University of Vietnam), seat of the Centre for Natural Resources and Environmental Studies (CRES), our main institutional research partner in the north. Dalat, the capital of Lam Dong province, is some 6 h by road from the southern metropolis, Ho Chi Minh City (HCMC), or, more precisely, from the University of Agriculture and Forestry (UAF) (now called the College of Agriculture and Forestry) in Thu Duc, our main institutional research partner in the south.

The specific objects of study

Once our choice of the two provinces had been made, we had to identify the specific objects of study, or rather, to be more accurate, the major elements to be measured over time and space. These were land use; population distribution; transport infrastructures, particularly roads; forestry activities; and biodiversity. However, such measurements had to be diachronic, rather than static. The central methodological objective was therefore to juxtapose the results of these measurements, relying on a multitemporal cartographic representation of each of these specific objects, or themes. The first one, land use, had to include forest land as well as agricultural land. Finally, we thought it would be useful to represent, if possible, more stable phenomena as well, such as landforms.

In any case, mapping had to be central to our approach. This would allow us to correlate the process to be explained (namely, the changes in forest cover, in terms of both area and type of forest) with the conditions and factors involved. Because biodiversity is one of the forest's major characteristics and one of its major assets, the measurement of its depletion also seemed important to us, both as an additional illustration and as an unfortunate consequence of the retreat of the forest.

Some clarifications

So far, I have used the phrase "the retreat of the forest," knowing full well that the term *retreat* is vague. In fact, it would be preferable to distinguish between degradation and deforestation. Degradation is the process whereby a forest gradually and slowly deteriorates through loss of biomass and biodiversity. Although it is being degraded, a forest may still be the major form of land use in a given area, but it is losing ground — it whittles away. When this loss of ground reaches 90% or more of the area previously covered by forest, the term *deforestation* is fully applicable. Thus, when I write of the retreat of the forest, I refer to a process that leads to the total or nearly total clearance of the forest, hence to deforestation.

Furthermore, available data do not allow for the measurement of anything but deforestation.

In our study, an additional element — a protagonist, one might be tempted to say — is, as already implied, the object of frequent misunderstandings and ambiguous statements, as much in the scientific literature as among politicians. This is slash-and-burn cultivation. This type of cultivation may take several forms, and the confusion surrounding these generates gross misinterpretations of the factors and processes involved in the retreat of the forest. It should be pointed out that, in strict terms, a slashed-and-burned field, or swidden field,[7] is an area cleared of its forest cover by fire, with the intention of this activity generally being to put the land to agricultural use. It may even be an area that was covered only with brush and grass. Thus, the terms *slash-and-burn cultivation* and *swidden agriculture* generally refer to an agricultural land use relying on fire for land clearance, whether that land was originally covered with trees, bushes, scrub, or grass.

Setting the vegetation cover on fire is an essential component of a practice some consider characteristic of agriculture in the humid tropics.[8] Such swidden agriculture is or was practiced by ethnic minorities in Viet Nam and in most other countries in the region. Almost everywhere, swidden agriculture relies on a succession of cultivation periods lasting 2 or 3 years at the most and fallow periods lasting 10–15 years, if not more. Furthermore, and this is an essential component of the system, the soil is never plowed, to avoid jeopardizing the forest cover's postagricultural regrowth; quite rightly, this is considered essential to the eventual renewal of the soil's fertility, which is indispensable to the cultivation of crops. A number of conditions determine the respective durations of these two forms of land use, particularly that of the fallow period, which allows for the partial reconstitution of the original forest cover. These conditions include the types of soils and types of crops; the specific techniques used; the nature of the landforms and, even more important, of the slopes; and local as well as regional demographic pressure. This sequence in land-use allocation — which can be referred to as a rotation of fields, rather than of crops — may at times necessitate the actual migration or relocation of the populations involved; the people move with their fields,

---

[7]The French terms used to designate swidden fields, *essart* or *brûlis*, are somewhat less confusing. Throughout Southeast Asia, numerous local terms serve to designate such fields and the tools and techniques related to them (Condominas 1957; Conklin 1961; Spencer 1966; Haudricourt 1974; Boulbet 1975).

[8]See, for example, Gourou's (1953) *The Tropical World*, the first edition of which appeared in French in 1947 (*Les pays tropicaux*) (Gourou 1947a). This book, a classic in the literature on the tropics, has been translated into several languages and has gone through several editions.

so to speak, so as not to distance themselves too much. But such displacements are not systematic and may in fact be relatively rare, especially when the overall forest realm available for the swidden cultivators' settlement is large enough to accommodate a well-balanced and nearly perpetual rotation of fields.[9] In that case, the term *shifting cultivation* refers primarily to the shifting or displacement of fields and secondarily to that of the populations practicing this.

This traditional form of agriculture, at times referred to as "rotational shifting cultivation," is fundamentally different from that practiced by peasants who cut down and burn the forest so that they can permanently cultivate the land and who, therefore, generally plow it. In fact, these cultivators, usually pioneering peasants or recent settlers, do not really practice swidden agriculture; they just make use of slash-and-burn land-clearing techniques to definitely transform *sylva* into *ager*, forest into field.

When applied to certain types of forest environment, particularly in mountainous terrain, this practice often leads to a gradual and at times rapid deterioration (over a period as short as 2 or 3 years) of the soil cover and to a decrease in its fertility. This then leads the pioneering peasants to abandon the land, leaving it barren, and to clear additional land at the expense of the forest. The expression *pioneer shifting cultivation*, generally used to designate this technique of agricultural expansion, is therefore quite inadequate because the actual process is not one based on shifting cultivation: the cultivated fields are not meant to be rotated; rather, they are just used intensively and excessively cropped and, shortly thereafter, discarded. This practice is usually carried out by pioneering peasants, who are generally quite poor but whose number has increased over the last decades throughout Southeast Asia, notably in Viet Nam. These colonists become both the tools and the beneficiaries (as limited as the ensuing benefits may be) of agricultural expansion, regardless of whether it is officially condoned, or even sponsored, by the state. This form of pioneering agriculture, wrongly called swidden agriculture, is occasionally practiced by members of minority ethnic groups, particularly the Hmong, who do push back the forest, at times for their own ends but, increasingly, as territorial spearheads of the advancing Kinh pioneers (see Chapter 5).

Finally, a third clarification appears necessary. Even before we began the analysis and interpretation of the retreat of the forest in the two selected provinces,

[9]For a community relying mainly on swidden agriculture to be able to settle in one location on a nearly permanent basis, the actual territory submitted to the fire–cultivation–forest-reconstitution cycle must lie around the actual settlement or at least be nearby. However, those who actually tend the fields must travel distances that increase with the size of the community, if they wish to maintain the necessary time-tested fallow period. This in turn may require the swidden cultivators to move closer to the fields temporarily, during the usually short peak-work periods. But in such instances, the home settlement remains stable.

we fully understood that the results would not be applicable to every region of Viet Nam. For example, the processes involved in the destruction of the Mekong Delta mangrove forests are not entirely similar to those that prevail in the Central Highlands. Nevertheless, analyzing a number of processes of which only some are active at the scale of the whole country seemed useful if only in terms of the contribution this would make to the development of research methodology.

Methodological objectives and training objectives

One of the main purposes of the project was to teach a research method that is not known in Viet Nam, namely, the hypothetico-deductive approach. Communist ideology and the training received by numerous Vietnamese intellectuals in the universities of the former Eastern bloc, mainly in the Soviet Union, apparently left a lasting imprint on the conception of scientific disciplines, particularly those dealing with society and territory. Each one — whether it is history, geography (physical or human), ethnology, sociology, economics, political science, business administration, or other — tends to operate behind closed doors, in total isolation from the others. In addition, for several decades now, Viet Nam has more or less functioned in a permanent state of urgency, if not crisis: research must generate quick answers, simple and clear and of a kind to allow for immediate action. For these reasons, social-science research in Viet Nam has essentially aimed to confirm certitudes, rather than to test hypotheses using empirical methods the parameters of which are defined to enable researchers to test those hypotheses.

Also, a large number of government and paragovernment departments, agencies, and institutions in Viet Nam are all involved in one form or another of research; rather than collaborating, these institutions tend to compete, particularly for the meagre financial resources that the country can afford to allocate for research. This situation is even worsened, paradoxically, by the involvement of international organizations and foreign institutions, whose number has been growing incessantly over the last few years. These frequently compete among themselves — even when they emanate from a single country (France, for example). They play into the hands of local researchers, who more often than not define both the objectives and the methods of their research according to priorities defined by the foreign sponsors and to the actual budgets the sponsors allocate.

Furthermore, it must be recognized that for some 40 years (1940–80) Viet Nam endured numerous conflicts and wars, with disastrous consequences for its national archival and documentary heritage. More than in most countries (but not more than in Cambodia), a document, a map, or a statistics table may fetch a lot of money, even if its origin is unconfirmed. Consequently, scientific research is strongly biased toward opportunism and empiricism, which makes it very difficult to carry out rigorous research that respects all the paradigms and objectives identified in the initial strategy. Finally, the validity and accountability of the research procedures eventually followed are rarely commensurate with the remarkable energy and resourcefulness deployed by Vietnamese researchers in their country-wide gathering of vast quantities of empirical data.

Let me be clear: my intention is not to lay blame on a given category of persons or institutions but to emphasize that in Viet Nam, perhaps more than in most countries, a transversal, multidisciplinary research project such as ours may lead to dispersal and waste of efforts and therefore warrants frequent reappraisals and readjustments, as well as repeated training and brainstorming sessions.

The research carried out and the problems encountered

Our initial research proposal, concerning the deforestation issue in Viet Nam, was submitted to the International Development Research Centre (IDRC) in October 1991. From November 1991 to November 1993, several meetings and workshops were held for the representatives of the four major institutions that were to be eventually involved in the collaborative research. These were CRES, attached to the University of Hanoi; the Centre for Socio-Economic Geography, a component of the National Centre for Social Sciences (NCSS), also based in Hanoi; the UAF, based in Thu Duc, an outer suburb of HCMC; and, finally, Laval University. These gatherings provided the opportunity not only to define, discuss, and redefine the objectives but also to make a choice among various possible empirical-research strategies. The research strategy had to be adapted to the problem and to the regions where the surveys were to be carried out and had to be understood and applied similarly by the research teams in Tuyen Quang and Lam Dong. The final proposal was submitted to IDRC at the end of 1993 and formally approved on 31 March 1994. Shortly afterward, the actual research project began.

During the 2 years of the project's implementation, from May 1994 to May 1996, a number of activities were carried out: meetings; training seminars, including long-term ones; empirical research, including data-collecting fieldwork; data analysis; mapping; interpretation; and drafting of results. Throughout the entire project, reliance on cartographic sources, tools, and means of representing and analyzing the objects of study remained central to our research approach and procedures.

But we also had to continue to devote much time and effort to discussions concerning the objectives of the project and the means to pursue them. These debates proved necessary for several reasons, including the following two: first, a large number of persons were involved in the project, many seemingly not very interested in understanding its objectives; second, a large number of documents and data considered indispensable to the "ideal" implementation of the research turned out to be nonexistent, impossible to find, or too costly, given the marketability of the supposedly public documents. To these problems should be added a third, one that actually encompasses the first two: it could be called difficulties in communication, whether verbal or written, between people and between places — the places of residence of the various members of the research team as well as the research sites.

Thus, from the beginning of the project until its completion, considerable energy was devoted to consultations, discussions, and debates. These were facilitated by numerous informal meetings between the various research partners, in Viet Nam as well as in Canada, and by seminars, workshops, and even conferences, mostly held in Viet Nam. The first objective of these seminars, workshops, and conferences was an assessment of our recent research accomplishments, but on every occasion we had to restate and explain the research objectives, as at every gathering it was clear that several of the Vietnamese research partners had somehow forgotten them. That seemed to explain why so many dispersed research initiatives were being undertaken, several of them having little to do with their stated objectives even though these had been clearly formulated at the outset and reiterated at every meeting. Nevertheless, on these occasions, a considerable number of research reports and papers, including maps, were presented.

The production of relevant cartographic documents was central to our research plan. It was also a crucial component of the training program, our intention being, as clearly stated at the outset of the project, to train our Vietnamese partners in the field of cartography. As the research made progress, the need to rely on cartographic representations took on added significance, as these maps seemed to provide the best means to illustrate and analyze eloquently and irrefutably the central phenomena, namely, deforestation and its presumed causes.

To this end, during September 1994, a Canadian researcher, Yann Roche, was posted to Viet Nam to monitor a series of training sessions, during which our Vietnamese partners were exposed to the basics of computer mapping.[10] Several workshops were held under his supervision, both in Hanoi and in HCMC, with some researchers from the northern team attending the southern workshops and vice versa. This initiative turned out to be one of the most successful of the entire project: most of the 10 or so Vietnamese researchers who attended these training sessions made notable and lasting progress in the field of computer cartography.

---

[10]Throughout the project, this researcher continued to monitor the project's cartographic production, especially during the 5-month interdisciplinary training undertaken at Laval University by four of our Vietnamese partners in 1995.

During the months that preceded these workshops, some preliminary data had been obtained, mostly from government departments and agencies involved in some form of forest planning, management, monitoring, exploitation, or protection.[11] Most of the data collection was handled by the Vietnamese members of the research team. The Canadian director of the project, along with research assistants (Vietnamese and Canadian), also visited and consulted with several local forestry officials in the provincial capitals and at the district levels. We were then able to discover that surprisingly little cooperation occurred between the various government agencies. And there was hardly any coordination regarding documentation, whether survey reports, statistics, airphotos, or maps. For example, in May 1994 and May 1995 in the town of Tuyen Quang, we visited the neighbouring offices of two forestry agencies — distinct but clearly complementary (or at least meant to be) — and found they neither shared nor exchanged any information.

In September 1994, a regional workshop was held at Thu Duc's UAF. This was followed in December by a much larger one in Hanoi and a regrouping of the leading researchers from the northern and southern teams. Results of the first 6 months of work were the topic of some 20 presentations, most backed by written papers. Several of these presentations were apparently based on vast amounts of data; a few were based on some quite remarkable maps, particularly those prepared by representatives of the Forest Inventory and Planning Institute (FIPI). Unfortunately, nearly all presentations revealed that very little consultation had been carried out between the northern and southern researchers, at least as far as actual empirical research was concerned. Consequently, although comparative interpretation was one of our research goals, it was impossible to carry out. In addition, the southern researchers applied a relatively clear and complementary division of research responsibilities and initiatives, but such was not the case among the northern team members, whose data-collection results were to a large degree marred by confusion. Finally, the research objectives remained largely misunderstood by a majority of the northern and southern team members, some of whom had quite evidently begun to prepare for the national workshop only a few days, if not a few hours, before the workshop.

In any case, having more or less botched their research mandate, several participants concluded, without providing the slightest evidence, that the ethnic minorities had to bear most of the responsibility for the ongoing deforestation of Viet Nam. During the conference, statements to that effect were solemnly made by participants who had never actually set foot inside any of the mountainous

[11] In Viet Nam, such institutions are so numerous that we were unable to identify them all, at least not clearly.

regions occupied by ethnic minorities. Consequently (because one of the objectives of this project was to train the Vietnamese researchers in the hypothetico-deductive method), once again we had to invite the participants to return to their homework, reminding everyone of what had been repeatedly stated since the outset of the project in May 1994, namely, the need to demonstrate before drawing any conclusions and the utmost unreliability and irresponsibility of making judgmental statements without any supporting evidence. The objectives of the project were, once again, formally listed, and so were recommendations about the methods to be used in pursuit of these objectives. These included, first, measuring deforestation over time; second, formulating, adjusting, or reformulating hypotheses about its possible causes; third, trying to measure the possible causes; and fourth, analyzing and interpreting the link or the absence of a link between deforestation and its possible causes.

In addition to this lack of understanding of the objectives to be pursued and the methods to be followed, we ran into two other problems: first, several of the researchers were unable to devote the time needed to execute their research mandate; second, it became increasingly evident that it would be most difficult to get our hands on many of the documents and data needed to test our hypotheses.

We then agreed to focus our data search on the 1975–95 period, but without giving up on our objective of covering a half century (1945–95). In addition, given the evident need to provide our Vietnamese research partners with better training and to incite them to consult one another more systematically on their common research ventures, we decided to send four of them to Laval University to attend a training program. In January 1995, the four selected trainees arrived in Quebec for a 5-month period. Two of these trainees came from the UAF; one came from CRES; and one came from NCSS. During their stay, the four Vietnamese researchers attended courses in forestry, public policy, and geography (with an emphasis on geographic information systems). Meanwhile, in Viet Nam, other members of the team pursued data collection in the northern research area and even more so in the southern one. In addition, we carried out map-digitizing tasks jointly, in Viet Nam and in Quebec. From then on, the acquisition and application of digitizing skills became a major component of our activities, especially in terms of time consumed. This turned out to be the case because the topographic, administrative, or thematic maps from which we had to extract basic data were made available to us at various scales. Furthermore, the work was made particularly complex by the numerous and frequent modifications that had been made to the administrative divisions of the country, for example, those concerning several districts and communes in Lam Dong province (Figure 4; see also Figure 15).

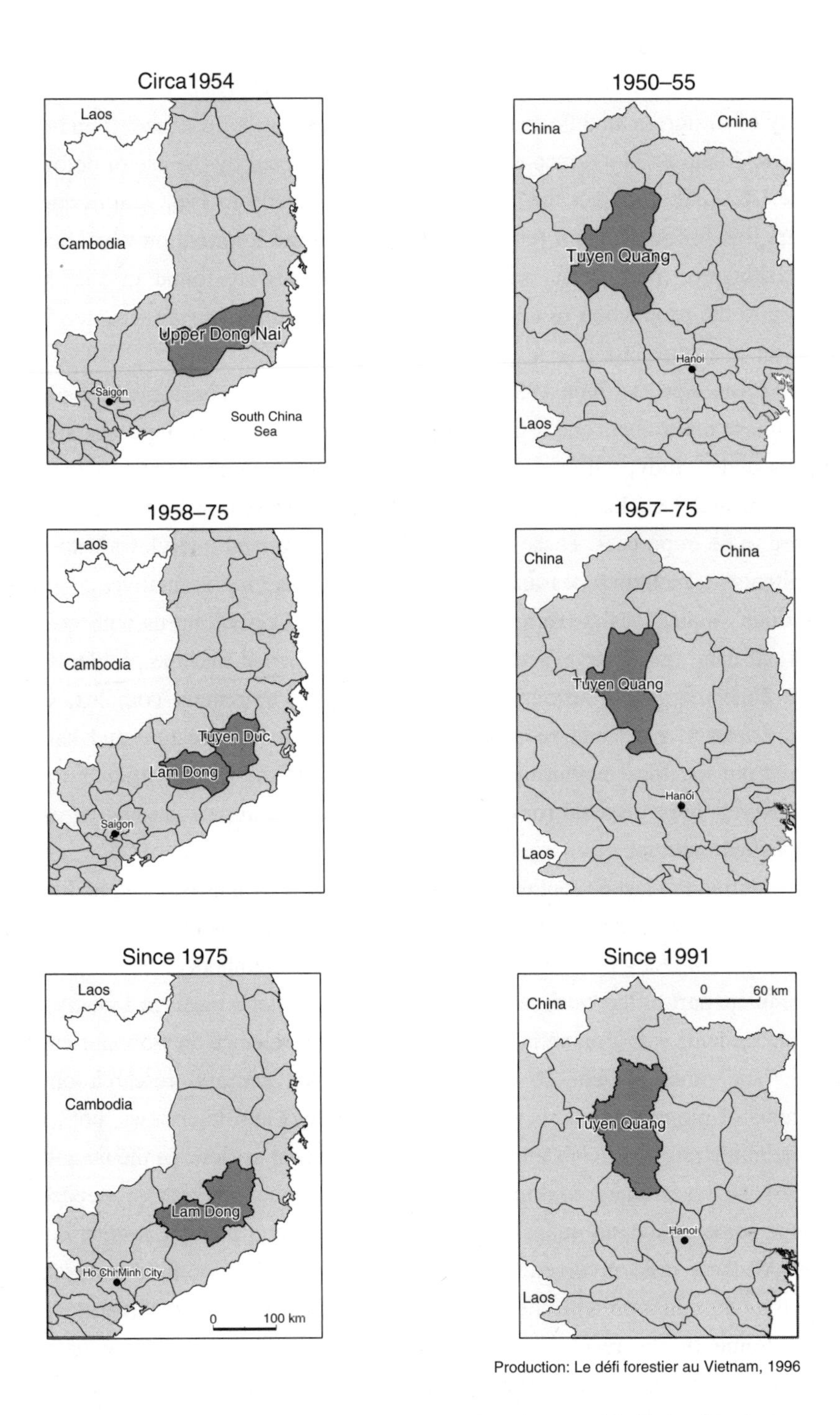

Figure 4. Some changes in the administrative units in Viet Nam: the cases of the North and the Centre.

The search for documents that would allow us to measure the presumed causes of the retreat of the forest even involved a trip to Washington by one of the Canadian research assistants to visit the National Archives at College Park, the Library of Congress, and Fort Belvoir. We were looking for documents and maps that would help us plot a map showing the areas affected by the use of defoliants by the US Air Force over the Central Highlands, mostly in 1968 and during the 4 years that followed. As it turned out, although some information was obtained in Washington, more useful sources of information were found in Viet Nam, leading to the production of a sketchy yet very relevant map (see Chapter 5 and the inset in Figure 20).

From April to June 1995, the project's director, accompanied by several Vietnamese researchers and a Canadian one, made a number of field visits in the regions under study, with side trips to the respective neighbouring provinces of Vinh Phu and Dac Lac, where comparable and related forms of deforestation seemed to be in process. These surveys led to meetings and interviews with local inhabitants — including peasants, pioneer peasants, and representatives of ethnic minorities — and local government officials. Besides providing us with specific empirical data, these surveys and observations confirmed that the problems and stakes concerning and surrounding the forests were extremely complex. Once again, however, clear and reliable documentary sources were rare and hard to obtain from the local authorities, even though all of the senior officials had at their discretionary disposal (or so it seemed) an indeterminate amount of useful unpublished material.

During the last 6 months of 1995 and the first 4 months of 1996, additional field research was carried out. In early 1996, two Laval students completed field surveys in Lam Dong province, with the assistance of members of the UAF team. To complete part of the work required to prepare a master's thesis in forestry, one of these students was looking into local communities' reliance on wood for energy needs. The other student, to complete part of his doctoral research on the dynamics of pioneer fronts, began a series of surveys and interviews, both with local administrative officials and with the new or recent settlers. In the meantime, Vietnamese researchers continued to collect data, including those needed to produce some of the key maps, such as the land-use and population-distribution maps. All these tasks involved the close collaboration of all the field researchers, as well as consultation with the members of the team working at Laval.

Some of the results were presented and discussed at a large national workshop, once again held in Hanoi, in early May 1996. Finally, during June and July, two of the Vietnamese research partners — one from Hanoi and the other from HCMC — came to Laval and worked with several of the Canadian team members to classify the documents and compile the data collected during the field-research phases and to analyze and interpret the major results.[12] This included the preparation of the computer cartography files, a task that had to be continued for a few more months, almost until the very end of 1996.

Before I present the results obtained and the lessons learned from the research, it is necessary to emphasize that we had to deal with three main problems:

- The perception and understanding that Vietnamese scholars and intellectuals tended to have of scientific research, particularly in the social sciences;

- The difficulties in communication — all forms of communication — within Viet Nam and between Viet Nam and the rest of the world, difficulties that would limit anyone's capacity to achieve original and reliable research results; and

- The prevailing attitude in Viet Nam regarding access to the documents and data (statistics, maps, etc.) needed to accomplish solid policy-oriented research — an attitude that, unfortunately, was too often mercantile or downright flippant. (Of course, foreign scholars are always properly and warmly hosted in Viet Nam, and it is important to underline that; but the problems of attitude and the methodological deadlocks that they entail render proper scientific enquiry extremely difficult and thus do the country a disservice.)

Nevertheless, the overall lessons and results of this interdisciplinary international-cooperation project were far from negligible. First, all the researchers demonstrated tremendous energy and acquired new skills, notably in the field of computer cartography and in terms of research epistemology and methodology. Second, beyond the professional improvements achieved by individuals, new and increasingly efficient modes of research collaboration were devised, involving researchers from several distinct scientific disciplines and coming from both a developed country, Canada, and a developing country, Viet Nam — countries

[12]These two researchers, Vo Thanh Son and Tran Dac Dan, were thus directly involved in the preparation of this final report.

unaccustomed to close cooperation with each other. Third, the primary objective of the project, namely, the proper initiation of interdisciplinary research, was in fact largely attained. Fourth, this allowed us to accomplish original, clear, and policy-relevant scientific results, as demonstrated in the following chapters.

Chapter 4
THE RESULTS FROM TUYEN QUANG PROVINCE

Tuyen Quang province (Figure 5) is located northwest of Hanoi and of the Red River delta, also known as the Tonkin Delta. Roughly rectangular, the province spreads over some 130 km from south to north, and its east–west width varies between 27 and 63 km (Figure 6). It actually belongs to the foothills of the Northern Highlands (the latter forming a broad crescent around the Tonkin Delta), and its own landforms rise, in a steplike manner, away from the lowlands (Figure 7). Whereas the southern portion of the province is made up of narrow river basins and of ranges of hills, most of which are below 300 m above sea level (asl), the average altitude rises in the northern portion, particularly in Chiem Hoa and Na Hang districts. Here, slopes are steeper, with several ranges reaching over 1 400 m asl. The two highest summits, rising to about 1 600 m asl, are located in Chiem Hoa district and in Son Duong district, near the neighbouring provinces of Vinh Phu to the south and Bac Thai to the east (see Figures 5 and 7).

In the southern part of the province, about 100 km away from Hanoi as the crow flies, is the provincial capital, also bearing the name of Tuyen Quang. This town is at an altitude of less than 100 m asl. From Hanoi, it can be reached by road in less than 5 h. This small town lies along the right bank of the Lo River (Song Lo), which originates in the northern neighbouring province of Ha Giang, near the Chinese border. A tributary to the Red River (which it joins farther south), the Lo River itself receives, north of Tuyen Quang and on its left flank, the waters of the Gam River (Song Gam). The valleys of these two rivers — the Lo and the Gam — represent the two major corridors running across the province, along a predominantly longitudinal axis.

According to the 1989 census, Tuyen Quang province held some 565 000 inhabitants. Given its surface area of 5 900 km^2, its population density stood at nearly 100 inhabitants/km^2 (see Table 3). It was estimated that, by 1997, its population would reach 660 000 people; and its density, about 110 inhabitants/km^2. This would still be largely below the national average of about 235 habitants/km^2. But, by 1992, even with a relatively low population density and a quite adequate

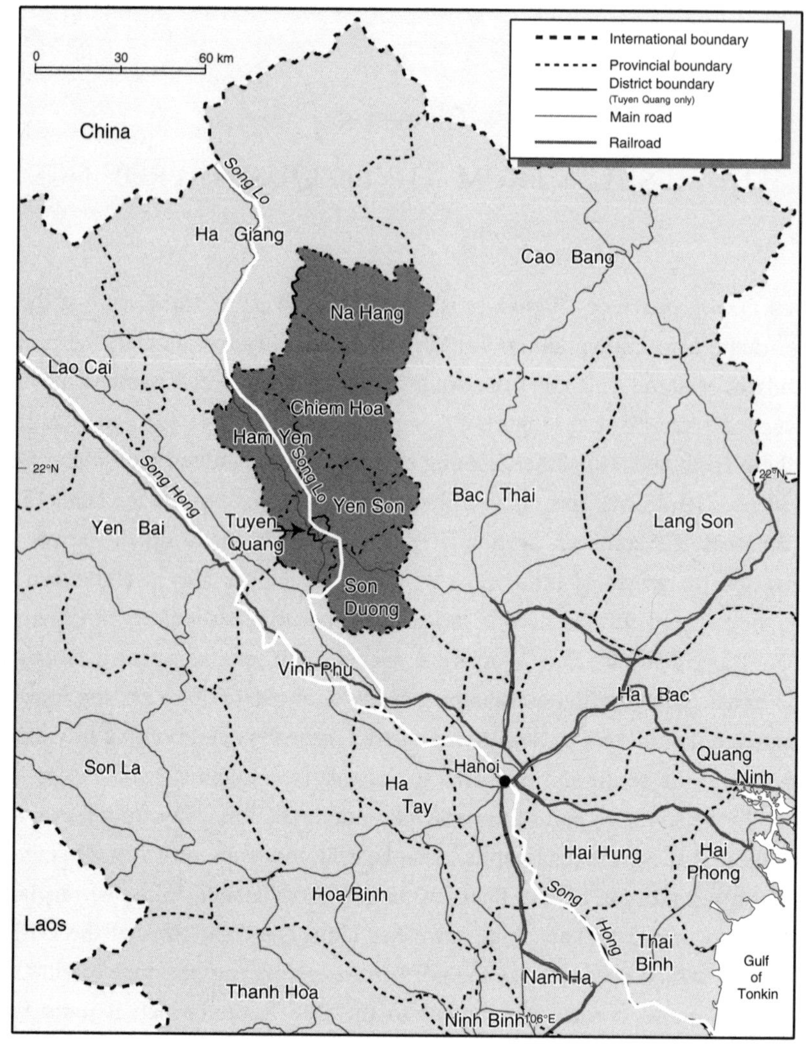

Production: Le défi forestier au Vietnam, 1996

Figure 5. Tuyen Quang province and its region since 1991.

annual rainfall (averaging between 1 400 and 2 000 mm), the province's natural forest, both rain forest and monsoon forest, covered only 7.2% of the province's territory (Figure 8; Table 5).[13]

---

[13]The sources that we consulted to piece together the land-use maps for 1975 and 1992 were based on various incomplete, contradictory, and at times confusing typologies. We therefore had to make choices and to rely on a much simplified typology. Thus, only one category (usually referred to here by the term *large closed forest*) was used to represent the two major forest types, rain forest and monsoon forest. We were, however, able to isolate a degraded form of forest cover, namely, the type in which bamboo predominates.

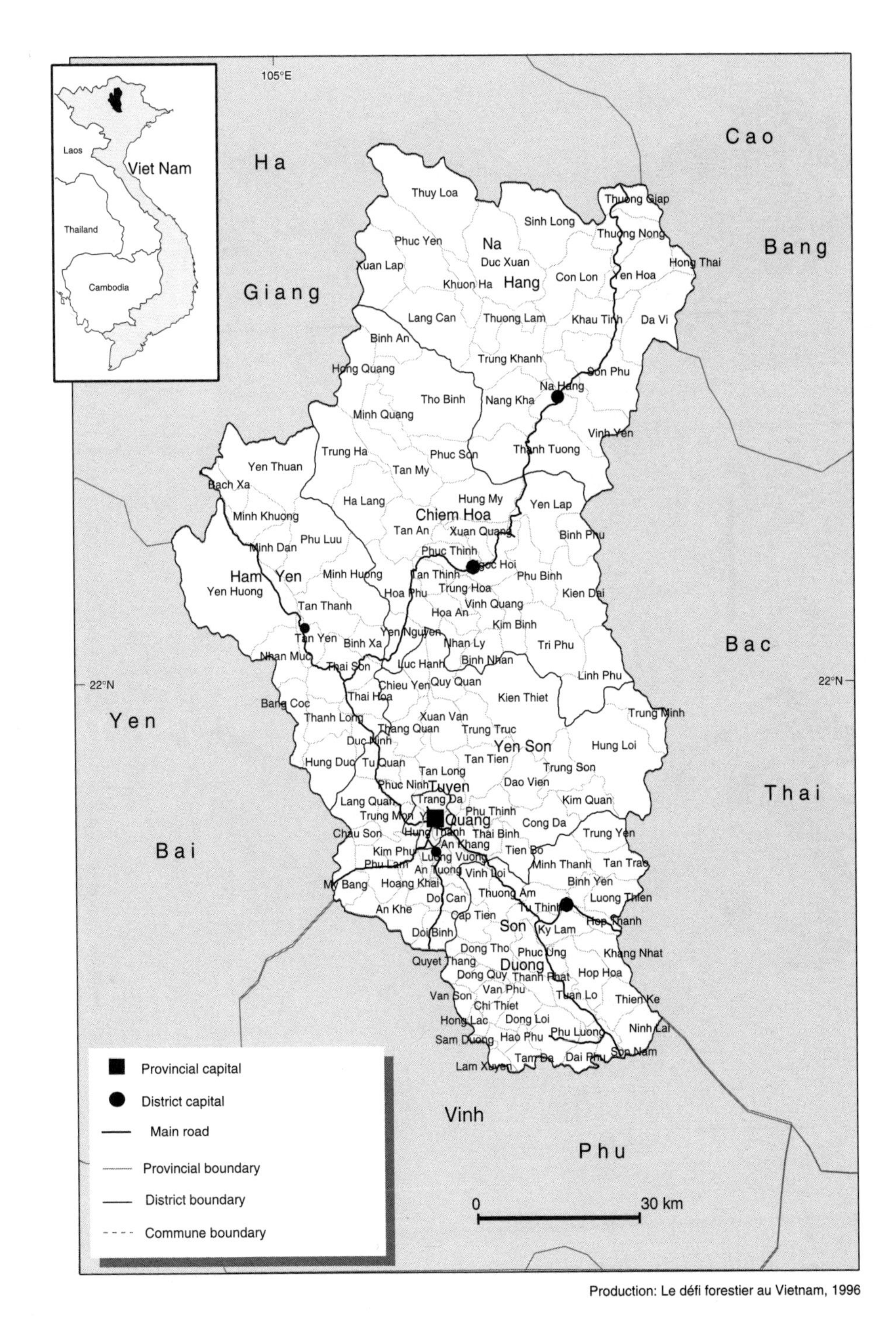

Figure 6. Tuyen Quang: administrative units. Source: Viet Nam Census Office, Hanoi (1989 census).

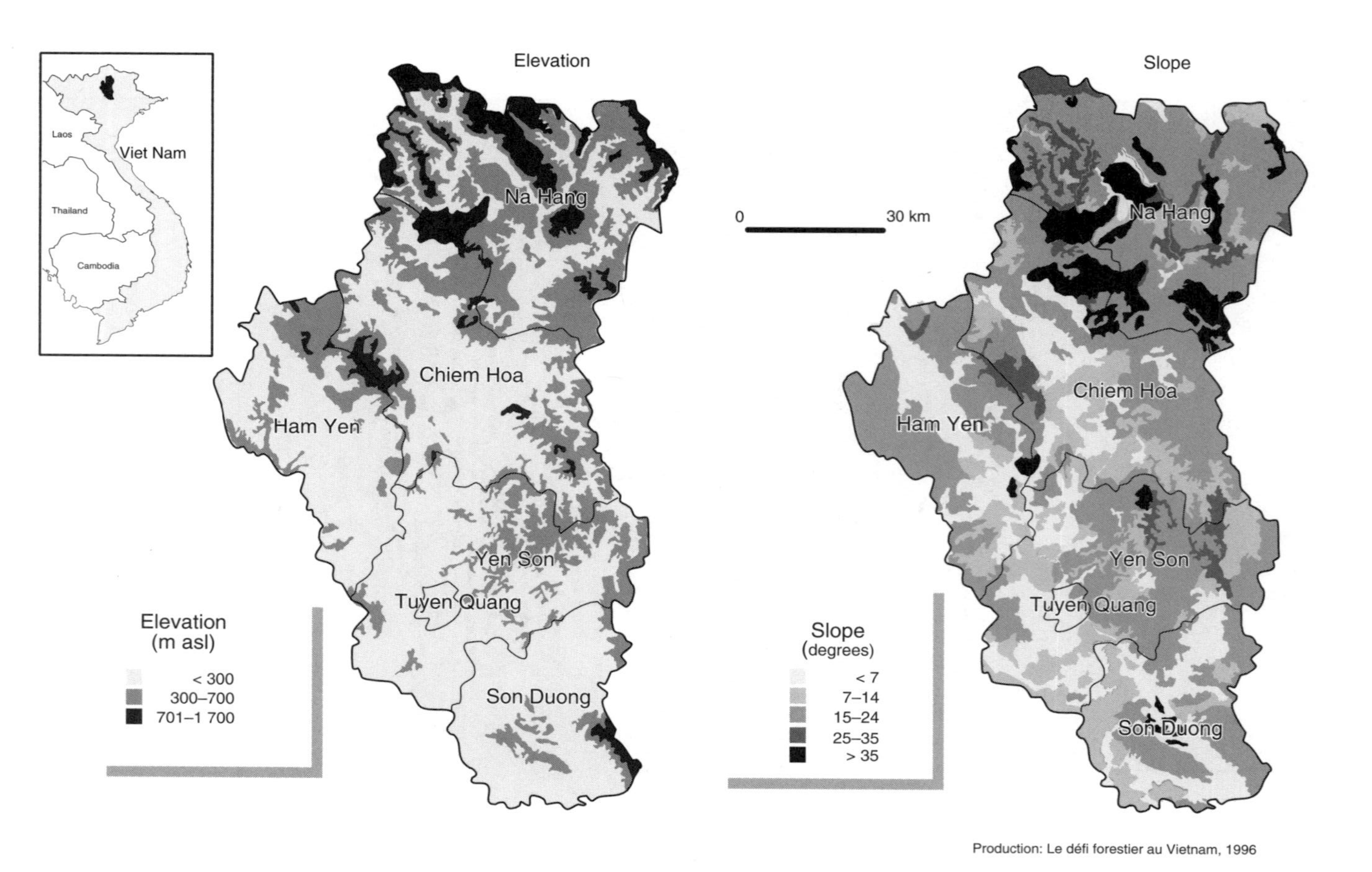

Figure 7. Tuyen Quang: elevation and slope. Source: Maurand (1943); Forest Inventory and Planning Institute, Hanoi, 1994. Note: m asl, metres above sea level.

Changes in land use

More than 50 years ago, P. Maurand, a French forestry engineer, put together a vegetation map of Indochina (Maurand 1943). Although it provides only very generalized information and does not allow for precise assessment of any specific forest type, it has nevertheless become a classic and basic reference on the forests of the Indochinese peninsula. According to the information presented on that map, some 90% of Tuyen Quang province was still covered with forest in 1943.[14] The map is reproduced here as an inset in Figure 8 for reference and heuristic purposes only, given that the land-use categories on which it was based (rich forest; average or poor forest; other) cannot be easily compared with those that have since been relied on. But this map does have the merit of, first, providing a striking illustration of the predominance of the overall forest cover in 1943 and, second, allowing for a partial comparison with maps made for 1975 and 1992, which are also presented in Figure 8, but at a better scale.[15]

The 1975 map

The 1975 map (see Figure 8) clearly shows that, as in 1943, the major agricultural areas were in the southern portion of the province, in the less mountainous Son Duong and Yen Son districts. (This, however, assumes that on the 1943 map the category "other" was referring first and foremost to agricultural land use.) An even more striking feature revealed by a comparison of the two maps is the magnitude of the retreat of the forest. By 1975, the large closed forests, whether rain or monsoon forests, covered barely 12% of the territory; bamboo forests, a degraded form of the former, covered about 16% (see Table 5).[16]

---

[14]This map and those showing land use for 1975 and 1992 (see Figure 8) were first processed by the FIPI, whose offices are located in the suburbs of Hanoi. Members of our research team subsequently submitted all these maps to a series of processes of simplification and standardization.

[15]We were able to put together a land-use map for 1982 as well. It was initially meant to be comparable with the 1975 and 1992 maps, but it quickly became evident that its contents were too imprecise and incoherent to allow for any meaningful analysis. Although it required hundreds of hours of work, as did the two others, we had to abandon the idea of making use of it.

[16]The surface areas covered by various land uses were determined by planimetry from the maps we produced. This ensures a perfect compatibility between our maps and our tables. It should be added that when the two figures we arrived at for areas covered by the large closed forests (12%) and by the bamboo forests (16%) are summed, the result (28%) is roughly equivalent to the figure often quoted by Vietnamese authors when they refer to the remaining "forest." This distinction is important because the so-called bamboo forest represents a very degraded form of tropical forest, whether of the rain-forest or the monsoon type. This degraded form may, however, over time and given favourable conditions, evolve toward a more advanced and richer form of forest, and eventually the climax type may be reconstituted.

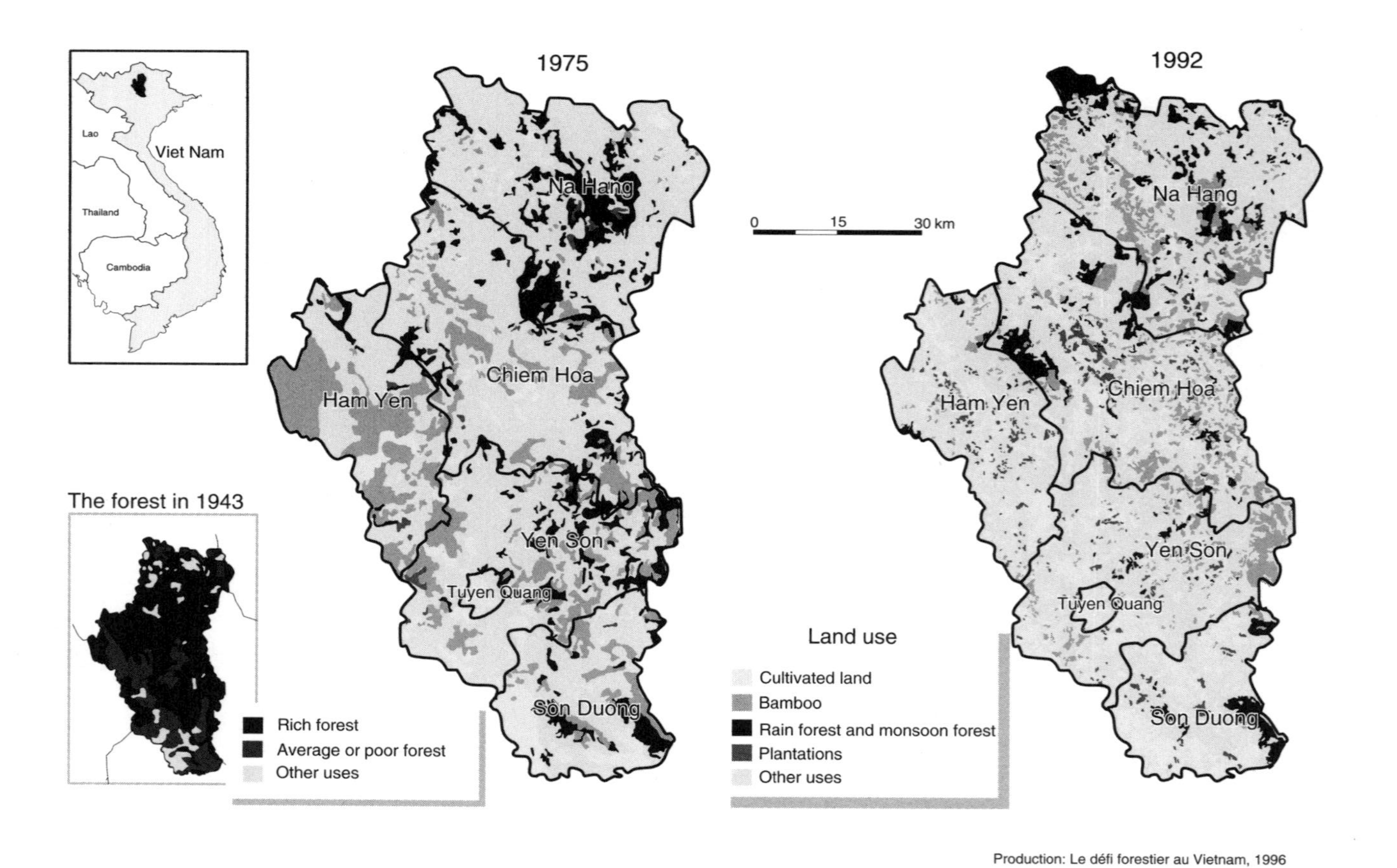

Figure 8. Tuyen Quang: changes in land use, 1975–92. Source: Maurand (1943); Forest Inventory and Planning Institute, Hanoi, 1994.

Table 5. Tuyen Quang province: changes in land use, by district, 1975–92.

	Cultivated land		Forest		Bamboo		Plantations		Other	
	(km^2)	(%)	(km^2)	(%)	(km^2)	(%)	(km^2)	(%)	(km^2)	(%)
1975										
Chiem Hoa	33	2.3	123	8.7	232	16.4	10	0.7	1 016	71.9
Ham Yen	44	4.7	37	3.9	371	39.6	6	0.6	480	51.2
Na Hang	36	2.4	297	20.2	3	2.2	12	0.8	1 092	74.3
Son Duong	173	21.4	90	11.1	110	13.6	1	0.1	436	53.8
Tuyen Quang [a]	20	46.5	2	4.7	0	0.0	0	0.0	21	48.8
Yen Son	75	6.1	160	13.0	224	18.2	10	0.8	762	61.9
Province	381	6.5	709	12.0	970	16.4	39	0.7	3 807	64.5
1992										
Chiem Hoa	264	18.7	126	8.9	170	12.0	38	2.7	816	57.7
Ham Yen	199	21.2	11	1.2	26	2.8	35	3.7	667	71.1
Na Hang	100	6.8	205	13.9	207	14.1	7	0.5	951	64.7
Son Duong	240	29.6	62	7.7	10	1.2	18	2.2	480	59.3
Tuyen Quang [a]	16	37.2	1	2.3	0	0.0	2	4.7	24	55.8
Yen Son	232	18.8	22	1.8	1 541	2.5	18	1.5	805	65.4
Province	1 051	17.8	427	7.2	567	9.6	118	2.0	3 743	64.5

Source: Figure 8.
[a] Municipality.

The 1975 map also shows that a third and apparently new feature — a new category of "land use," so to speak — had become predominant. This new category, applicable to more than 65% of the province, actually refers to denuded or barren lands, for it seems quite probable that, in this case, the "other" category does refer to such lands.[17] These basically correspond to areas cleared of their forest cover in such a way that regrowth appears most unlikely. They may have been sites of ephemeral cultivation that have been totally abandoned because of a rapid decrease in soil fertility.

Overall, within the province, the most pronounced differences in land use among the various districts are in the categories of cultivated land and forest (including bamboo forest). Permanent cropland appears essentially confined, as I have already mentioned, to the southern portion of the province, whereas the large closed forest is more characteristic of the northern districts and is still nearly twice as widespread (12% versus 6.5%). Although bamboo forest is nearly absent from Na Hang district, it is well represented throughout the other major districts.

The 1992 map

Several meaningful phenomena and processes are revealed by a comparison of the 1992 map with the 1975 one (see Figure 8). First, the area devoted to agriculture has noticeably increased, from 6.5% to almost 18% of total land use (see Table 5). Agricultural expansion occurred in all districts, but with a particularly striking intensity (from about 2% to almost 19%) in Chiem Hoa, although this is one of the more hilly and mountainous districts.

Second, bamboo forests in several districts have been replaced by other forms of land use, particularly agriculture but also barren land.

Third, barren lands have remained quite predominant, still accounting in 1992 for 64.5% of total land use. However, their actual distribution throughout the province seems to shift constantly.

Fourth, although in some places the large closed forests seem to have made some gains, overall they have continued to lose ground. The most important losses occurred in the most mountainous district, Na Hang, which is also the most northerly.

---

[17]Reference to this "other" land-use category can become confusing and misleading. In fact, it does illustrate the immense difficulty encountered by anyone trying to interpret Vietnamese maps. Having familiarized ourselves with the sources consulted for the production of the 1975 and 1992 maps, we became reasonably certain that the "other" category on the 1943 map served to designate agricultural lands, whereas the same category refers to uncultivated and nonforested rural areas on the 1975 and 1992 maps.

Fifth, the routes of agricultural expansion are quite evident from Figures 7 and 8, which show that such expansion occurs initially in the river basins and along the slopes of the lower foothills, as in the centre of Ham Yen.

Sixth, on both the 1975 and 1992 maps, the land-use category "plantation" is barely represented.

Changes in the population and its distribution

Over three decades, between 1960 and 1989, the province's population nearly quadrupled, increasing from about 154 206 to some 565 023 inhabitants (Table 6). This growth seems to have been sustained throughout the entire period, at least if it is broken down into two phases: 1960–75 and 1975–89. All districts were involved, in nearly equivalent fashion, with some minor differences.

First, the growth rate for the 1960–75 phase was slightly stronger, possibly because people fleeing the US bombing of the Red River delta were forced to migrate into the less industrialized peripheral and mountainous regions.

Second, the municipal district of Tuyen Quang itself, the provincial capital, met with the strongest rates of growth.

Third, the two southern districts of Son Duong and Yen Song had the largest population increase in absolute numbers, probably because they lie closer to the highly populated delta regions but also because their topography and soils are more favourable.

The available data — or rather, the available reliable data — did not allow us to determine what would have been the respective and relative shares of natural

Table 6. Tuyen Quang province: changes in population, by district, 1960–89.

	Population			Ratio		
	1960	1975	1989	1975 : 1960	1989 : 1975	1989 : 1960
Chiem Hoa	31 139	62 768	103 540	2.0	1.6	3.3
Ham Yen	18 129	44 326	81 857	2.4	1.8	4.5
Na Hang	19 804	33 187	50 944	1.7	1.5	2.6
Son Duong	34 404	83 605	140 366	2.4	1.7	4.1
Tuyen Quang [a]	9 987	32 094	47 982	3.2	1.5	4.8
Yen Son	40 743	80 113	140 334	2.0	1.8	3.4
Province	154 206	336 095	565 023	2.2	1.7	3.7

Source: Tuyen Quang Provincial Statistics Bureau.
[a] Municipality.

population growth and migrations in the overall population increase of the given districts. Some evidence indicates that, over recent years, outmigrations from the province have tended to largely compensate for, if not be equal to, inmigrations.

In any case, between 1960 and 1989, overall demographic growth was responsible for a corresponding increase in population densities, with the higher ones still found among the southern districts but showing a tendency to spread toward the northern, more mountainous districts. Maps representing the changes in population densities by commune (Figure 9) clearly illustrate the demographic filling-in process that took place, from the south of the province toward its centre and the north. As it turns out, it is precisely these areas that had, at least between 1975 and 1989, the most noticeable expansion in agricultural land use. As a result, the province's population gravity centre was displaced northward, moving closer to the mountainous areas, where forests are relatively more widespread and where the relative demographic weight of the ethnic minorities remains more important, although their integration is being speeded up.

The expansion of Kinh settlement

The population increase, which has led to more and more intensive settlement of the mountain districts, is clearly associated with the expansion of agriculture. It also seems to be closely linked with the progression of Viet or Kinh settlement. In fact, between 1960 and 1989, the increase in the number of Kinh, in comparison with those of the ethnic minorities, has manifested itself territorially. As is quite clearly illustrated by maps showing the changes in the proportion of Kinh in the population by commune, the Kinh's share has grown just about everywhere in the province.

The progression of this growth follows the northward expansion of agriculture, as well as the path of deforestation (Figure 10). Overall, for the whole of the province, from 1960 to 1975 and from 1975 to 1989, the proportion of Kinh in the total population grew from 39.8% to 47.9% and then to 52.6%. This relative increase occurred in all districts (Table 7).[18] A noticeable difference, in terms of rhythm, appears between the two periods; the first one (1960–75) witnessed stronger growth. Also during that period, as mentioned above, US bombardments of the Red River delta were responsible for waves of migrations toward the less industrialized peripheral and mountainous regions.

[18]Lam Thi Mai Lan, one of the NCSS researchers involved in the project, presented and analyzed these figures during the project's final workshop, held in Hanoi in May 1996.

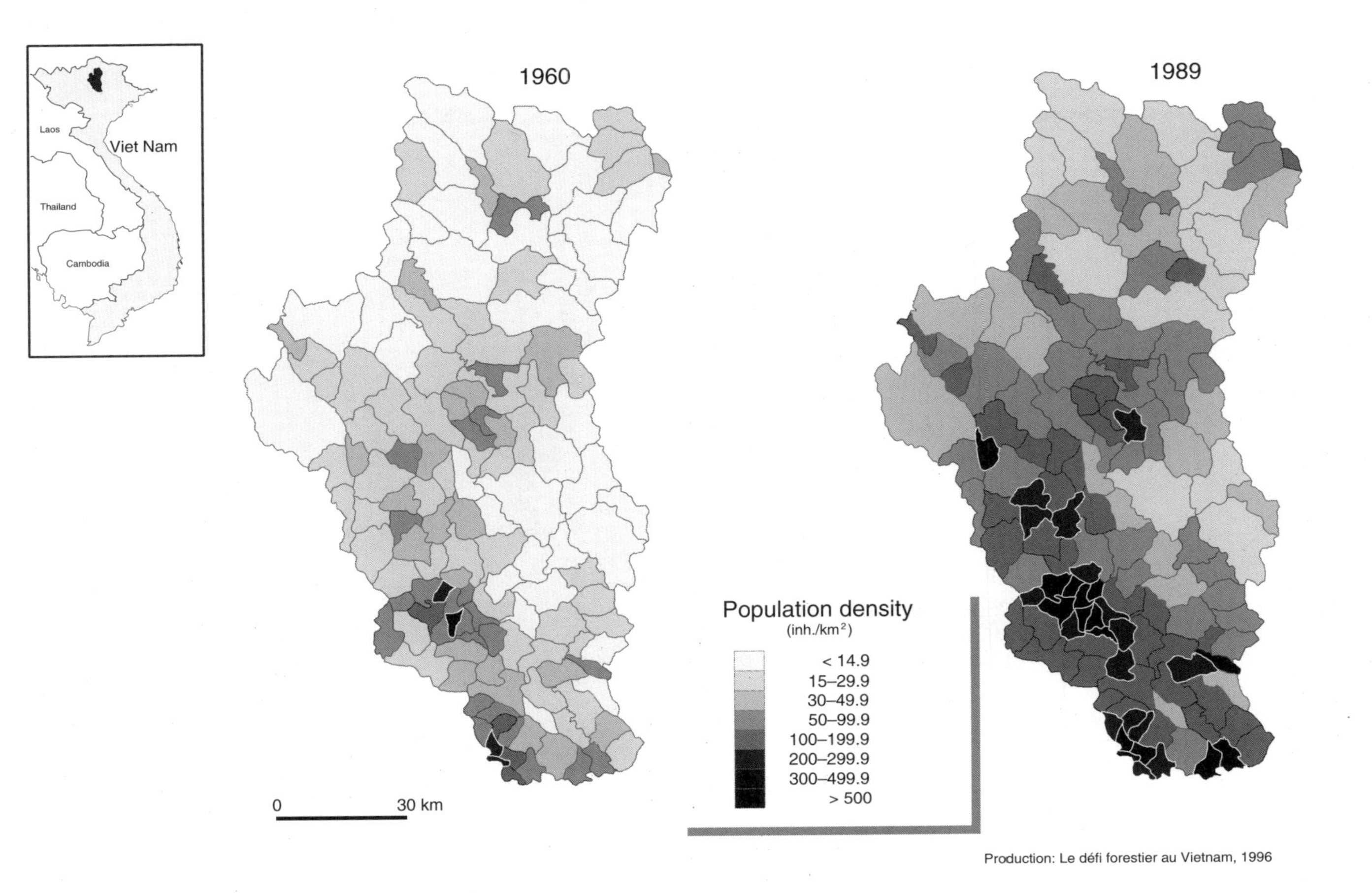

Figure 9. Tuyen Quang: changes in population density, by commune, 1960–89. Source: Department of Statistics, Viet Nam. Note: inh., inhabitants.

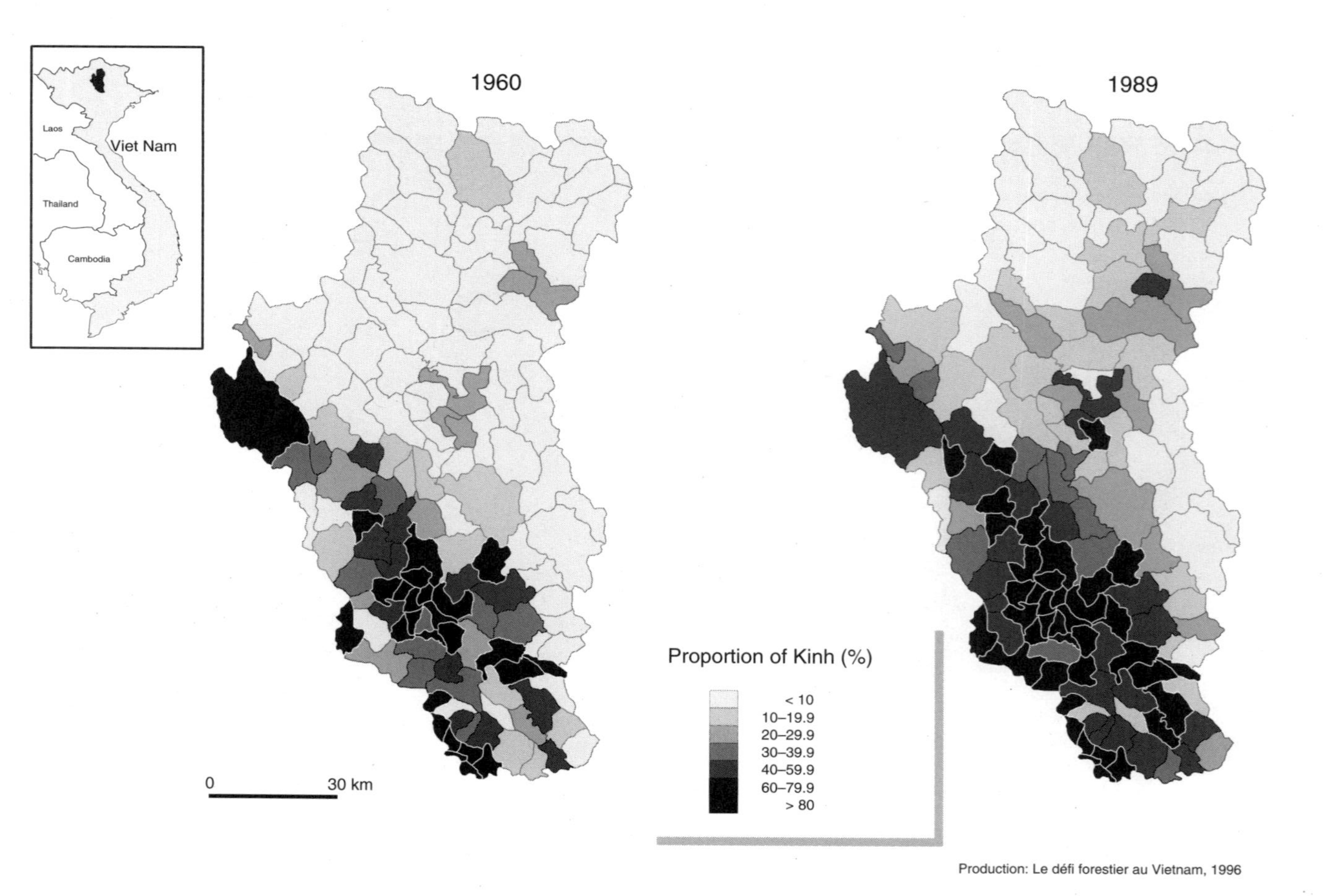

Figure 10. Tuyen Quang: changes in the proportion of Kinh in the population, by commune, 1960–89. Source: Department of Statistics, Viet Nam.

Table 7. Tuyen Quang province: changes in ethnic composition of the population, by district, 1960–89.

	Kinh–Muong (%) [a]			Tay–Thai and others (%)			Hmong–Yao (%)		
	1960	1975	1989	1960	1975	1989	1960	1975	1989
Chiem Hoa	10.9	23.3	25.6	75.5	65.1	62.9	13.6	11.5	11.6
Ham Yen	27.2	34.9	48.2	44.2	36.4	23.1	28.6	28.7	23.0
Na Hang	4.3	14.5	12.5	66.8	57.3	58.8	28.9	28.1	28.7
Son Duong	55.9	60.4	63.3	40.8	36.4	33.6	3.3	3.1	3.1
Tuyen Quang [b]	98.4	88.6	94.2	1.4	11.0	5.4	0.2	0.4	0.4
Yen Son	56.9	58.8	64.7	32.4	26.7	22.8	10.7	14.5	12.5
Province	39.8	47.9	52.6	46.8	39.1	35.5	13.4	13.0	11.9

Source: Tuyen Quang Provincial Statistics Bureau.

[a] It should be pointed out that, most likely, not a single Muong resides in Tuyen Quang province and that persons designated in the official statistical reports as Kinh–Muong are in fact all Kinh.

[b] Municipality.

Within Tuyen Quang province itself, the increase in the proportion of Kinh (Kinh–Muong in the official statistical reports)[19] in the total population is much more noticeable in the northern mountainous districts of Chiem Hoa, Ham Yen, and Na Hang. For example, in Ham Yen in 1960, the Kinh accounted for 27.2% of the district's total population, but by 1989 their share had reached 48.2%. In the even less densely populated districts of Na Hang and Chiem Hoa, the ethnic minorities, particularly the Tay–Thai, were still largely predominant in 1989. However, the decline of this predominance appeared to be well under way between 1960 and 1975, although it leveled off between 1975 and 1989 (see Table 7). Needless to say, these northern districts were those where most of the agricultural expansion, described earlier, took place (see Figure 8 and Table 5).

The expansion of Kinh settlement and the growth of the demographic share of the Kinh, from 39.8% to 52.6% between 1960 and 1989, occurred at the expense mostly of the Tay–Thai, whose own proportion of the province's total population dropped from 46.8% to 35.5%. This proportionate decline of the Tay–Thai population was particularly striking in Ham Yen district (44.2% to 23.1%). Also significant is that in 1960 the Tay–Thai were more numerous than the Kinh (46.8% versus 39.8%), but by 1975 and, even more, by 1989, the Kinh had largely taken over as the province's major ethnic group, accounting for 52.6% of the province's overall population, versus 35.5% for the Tay–Thai.

The Hmong–Yao's share declined slightly over the three decades in four districts but increased slightly in the other two, with a resulting modest decline at the provincial level, from 13.4% to 11.9% (see Table 7).

What about swidden agriculture?

The data and documents used to prepare the land-use maps did not allow us to really measure the impact of swidden agriculture on the forest cover or on the changes to the cover. However, according to information obtained at the provincial office of the Department of Statistics in the town of Tuyen Quang, this form of agriculture, as practiced by the ethnic minorities, concerned only 3 000 ha (30 km^2) in 1992.[20] Although the area affected by shifting cultivation increased somewhat during the 1980s, it has since apparently begun to decline. Because the

[19]It should be pointed out that, most likely, not a single Muong resides in Tuyen Quang province and that persons designated in the official statistical reports as Kinh–Muong are in fact all Kinh.

[20]Dan Duc Phuong, another of the NCSS researchers involved in the project, presented and analyzed these figures during the project's final workshop, held in Hanoi in May 1996.

Table 8. Tuyen Quang province: changes in firewood consumption, by ethnic group, 1960–89.

	1960		1975		1989	
	(t)	(kg/person)	(t)	(kg/person)	(t)	(kg/person)
Kinh	80 439	1 310	194 780	1 210	359 331	1 110
Tay–Thai	108 950	1 510	180 028	1 370	244 373	1 220
Miao–Dao	49 147	2 380	83 923	1 920	97 931	1 450
Total	238 536	1 547	458 731	1 364	701 635	1 242

Source: Tuyen Quang Provincial Statistics Bureau.

total area of the province devoted to agriculture is 1 051 km^2 (see Table 5), that is, nearly one-fifth of its total territory, this would mean that no more than 3% of it is submitted to shifting cultivation. Notwithstanding the incompleteness of the information on which this statement is based, it does seem to indicate that shifting cultivation cannot be considered a significant factor in the recent and rapid retreat of the province's forest cover.

And firewood?

Coherent statistical data concerning the reliance on firewood, particularly for cooking purposes, are equally hard to come by and must be used as cautiously as those concerning the ethnic minorities' agricultural activities. According to recent data, also obtained from the provincial office of the Department of Statistics, the consumption of firewood has been on the increase (Table 8).[21] But this increase in absolute quantity consumed can be entirely attributed to overall population growth, as per capita consumption has in fact significantly declined. Just as noticeable, however, is that the decline in per capita consumption has been much greater among the members of the ethnic minorities living in the uplands of the province than among the Kinh. Thus, although the per capita firewood consumption among the Tay–Thai and particularly among the Hmong–Yao was clearly higher than among the Kinh in 1960, it declined to such an extent among the minorities that the respective levels of consumption had become nearly comparable by 1989. Since then the number of Kinh has increased, in both absolute and relative terms, much more rapidly than the number of non-Kinh. The Kinh are therefore most

[21]Dan Duc Phuong also presented and analyzed these figures during the project's final workshop, held in Hanoi in May 1996.

likely to be primarily responsible for the massive threefold increase in firewood consumption over the three decades, from about 239 000 t to 702 000 t.[22]

As shown earlier, the increased Kinh presence was largely linked to agricultural expansion, particularly during the 1960s and 1970s. We could, therefore, formulate the hypothesis that the fundamental instrumental cause of the forest cover's degradation, even of its retreat, is agricultural expansion, to which is related a massive increase in firewood collection, which acts as an additional agent of forest degradation.

The impact of commercial logging

It is apparent to anyone traveling through Tuyen Quang province that commercial logging, carried out by state-sponsored enterprises, is also a major cause of deforestation. Such business concerns are either firmly established or at least very active in each of the districts. However, the one whose impact is most noticeable is the Bai Bang pulp and paper mill. Located on the right bank of the Lo River, in Vinh Phu province, just south of Tuyen Quang province, which is part of its hinterland (raw-material area), this mill is by far the largest of its kind in Viet Nam. Its construction and operation have been largely financed by Sweden. It began operating in the early 1980s.

Throughout the duration of our project, certain data on this pulp and paper mill were collected by several members of the project's research team.[23] However, the data, notably those concerning the supply of raw material, were not systematic enough to allow for a reliable cartographic representation of the raw-material area and of the changes over time. Such a representation would have allowed us to measure the mill's impact on the retreat of the forest in Tuyen Quang, as well as in the four surrounding provinces. Notwithstanding the various hinterland-replanting programs of some tree species (including several *Eucalyptus* spp. of lesser quality than those growing in the local natural forests), it appears that the mill has also been relying for its supplies on some not so clearly identified networks of intermediaries. These intermediaries are responsible for collecting the raw material from unofficial suppliers, who are, in fact, peasants in

---

[22]Two comments must be added here. Among the members of ethnic minorities, average income appears to be a great deal less than that of the Kinh; and in poor rural communities, it is the poorest among the poor who rely the most on the fuel of the poor, namely, firewood. The difference in respective per capita firewood-consumption levels of the Kinh and of the non-Kinh thus appears surprisingly low. Could this be attributed to a recent improvement in the minorities' living standards? Or could it be attributed to a wiser use of resources among these minorities? Answers to these questions could only be obtained through careful field surveys.

[23]In particular by Dan Duc Phuong, who presented reports on the Bai Bang pulp and paper mill at the December 1994 and May 1996 workshops.

dire need of the revenue from marketing wood (including bamboo harvested from the remaining patches of degraded forests bordering the agricultural areas). But all these processes have been insufficiently documented. In fact, it seems that over the last few years, most of Bai Bang mill's local supplies have come from the replanted areas managed by state enterprises.

One thing does seem certain: the impact of this pulp and paper mill on the region's forest cover has been significant. According to a recently published study (Lang 1997), between 1982 and 1992 some 90 000 ha of land was cleared of all trees to supply the mill.[24]

Finally, it is also quite evident that several forms of illegal logging are practiced in the region, although we have not been able to accurately measure the extent and impact of these practices.

The fate of the biodiversity

We were unable to carry out much original research in the field of biodiversity, although some specific research mandates to collect biodiversity data had been handed out. The information that was assembled was not available in a form that would have allowed us to relate the changes in biodiversity resources to the retreat of the forest cover and its presumed causes. However, some data were indeed compiled from various existing sources and reassessed by some of the Vietnamese researchers associated with the project.[25] Toward the end, a synthesis was drawn from the various documents assembled by these researchers, and this was submitted as one of the annexes contained in the final report. It included a reference to the presence within Tuyen Quang province of 90 families, 258 classes, and 597 species of flora, many of which are endangered.

Finally, again on the basis of the documents submitted by Vietnamese members of our team, it was possible to come up with a cartographic representation of the changes in population of several species of mammals (Figures 11 and 12). The first set concerns six species: the tiger, the Asiatic black bear, the clouded leopard, the Indian muntjak (a small cervine), the sambar (another small cervine), and the Sumatran serow (a small caprine) (Figure 11). The second set deals with three primates: the Tonkin snub-nosed monkey, François' monkey, and Phayre's leaf monkey (Figure 12).

[24]The history of the Bai Bang pulp and paper mill, along with the geography and even the geopolitics of the mill's impacts, would be a worthy topic for a doctoral dissertation.

[25]These included the paper presented by Professor Lam Xuan Sanh at both of the workshops held in December 1994 in HCMC and Hanoi, as well as the two papers presented by Dang Huy Huynh, Hoang Minh Khien, Le Xuan Canh, and Tran Van Thang during the December 1994 and May 1996 Hanoi workshops.

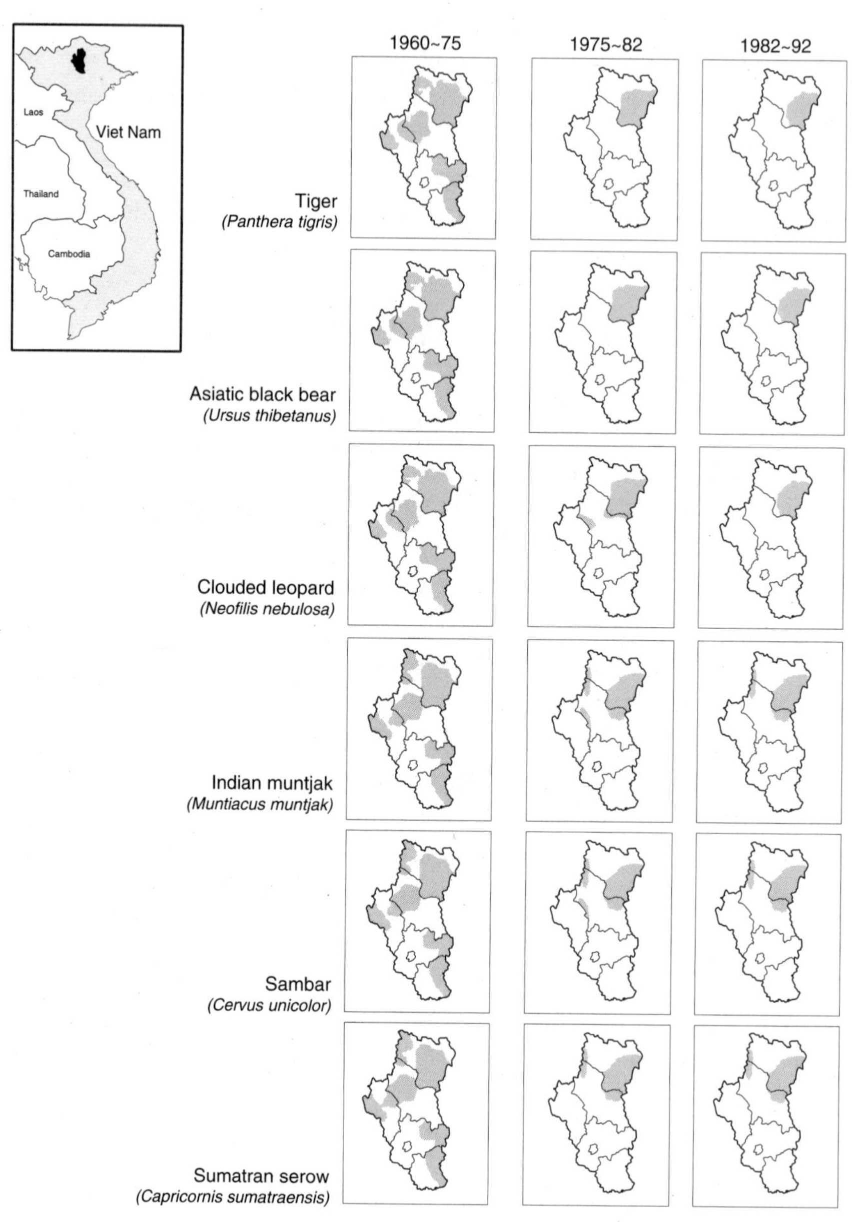

Figure 11. Tuyen Quang: changes in the distribution of six species of mammals, by district, 1960–92.

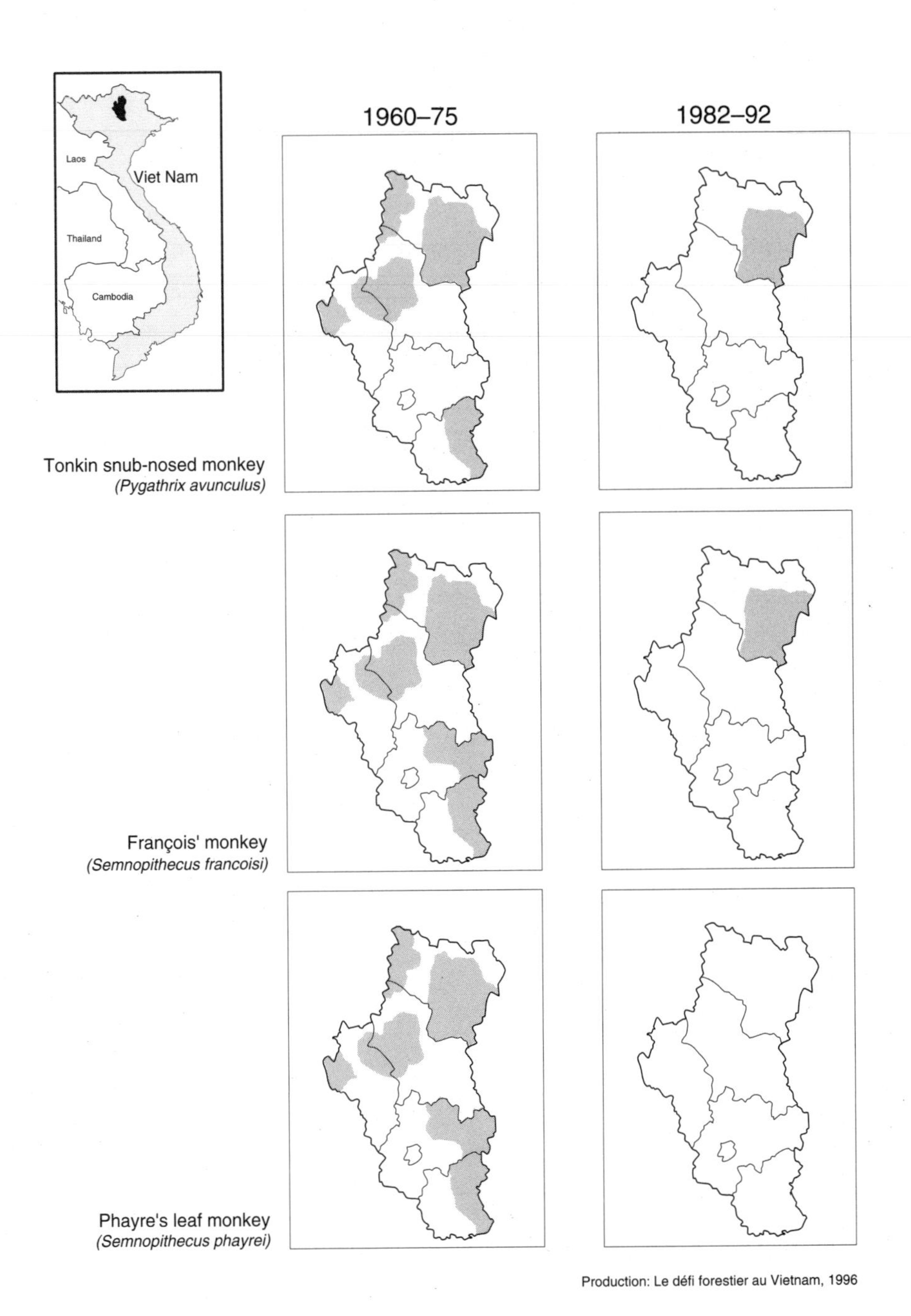

Production: Le défi forestier au Vietnam, 1996

Figure 12. Tuyen Quang:. changes in the distribution of three species of primates, by district, 1960–92.

Although assembled at a rather rough scale, these cartographic representations do illustrate the dramatic reduction of the habitat of each of these mammals. In fact, during each of the three periods represented — 1960–75, 1975–82, and 1982–92 — their respective territories appeared largely equivalent and in some cases absolutely identical. In other words, the territorial distribution of each of these species seems to have evolved in an similar manner. During the initial period (1960–75), tigers, bears, and panthers, as well as representatives of the six other species, were still to be found in each of the province's districts, except in the municipal district of Tuyen Quang. By 1992, the Phayre's leaf monkey had completely disappeared and the other eight species were confined to the northern mountainous districts of Chiem Hoa and Na Hang. In fact, five of these could only be found in Na Hang district: the tiger, the Asiatic black bear, the clouded leopard, the Tonkin snub-nosed monkey, and François' monkey.

In short, the habitat of each of these mammals is shrinking rapidly — as is their number — following the pace of the retreat of the forest, and this in turn appears to be dictated by agricultural expansion. I have already shown that for understandable reasons this expansion was first achieved along the lower slopes (see Figures 7 and 8). This explains why it is in areas of higher relief and steeper slopes that the last expanses of rain forest are to be found — along with the last of the mammals, which take refuge under the canopy.[26]

[26]This increasingly noticeable confinement of the province's last rain forests to the uplands and steep slopes was the topic of a paper presented by Duong Tri Hung, from FIPI, at the December 1995 Hanoi workshop.

Chapter 5

The results from Lam Dong province

Lam Dong province (Figures 13 and 14) belongs to the Tay Nguyen — literally, the "western mountains." This upland area, often called the Central Highlands or Central Plateaus, is located in the south-central interior of Viet Nam. The Kinh have long considered the Central Highlands as a land reserve that they hesitated to colonize until the 1920s — and then it was only at the urging of the French colonial authorities. Their reluctance was linked to a number of factors: the remoteness of Tay Nguyen from the traditional and densely populated coastal and deltaic settlements; the lack of access to, and transport through, these heavily forested uplands; and the perception that the region was inhospitable and constituted the domain, even the sanctuary, of the ethnic minorities. Among the more foreboding characteristics of these forest-covered highlands was malaria.[27]

Lam Dong is the southernmost of the four provinces belonging to Tay Nguyen; its own southern reaches tumble down toward Dong Nai province and the lowlands of Cochinchina. It is oriented southwest–northeast and is 175 km long, and its broadest section measures more than 65 km. Many of its summits surpass 2 000 m asl, and its capital, Dalat, is located in a 1 500-m-high basin surrounded by several peaks. Dalat is only some 300 km from HCMC, to which it is linked by a good road. The trip between the two cities, involving two mountain passes, can be completed in less than 6 h.

Although it has a noticeably larger area than Tuyen Quang province (more than 10 000 km^2 versus less than 6 000 km^2), Lam Dong province is not as densely populated (see Table 4). According to the 1989 census, its population stood at some 660 000 inhabitants, meaning a density of about 64 inhabitants/km^2 (versus 96 inhabitants/km^2 in Tuyen Quang for the same year). According to the estimates produced by the Vietnamese statistical services, Lam Dong's population had reached 733 000 inhabitants by 1992, and it can be estimated that by 1997 it had

[27]Starting in the 1930s, the French geographer Pierre Gourou repeatedly emphasized the extent to which malaria acted as a crucial demographic factor, that is, that it had a negative impact on the growth and territorial expansion of the population; see, for example, Gourou and Loubet (1934) and Gourou (1940, 1947a, b, 1953). Gourou and Loubet (1934) added that the highlands of Viet Nam were poorly endowed in terms of soil, but that was false.

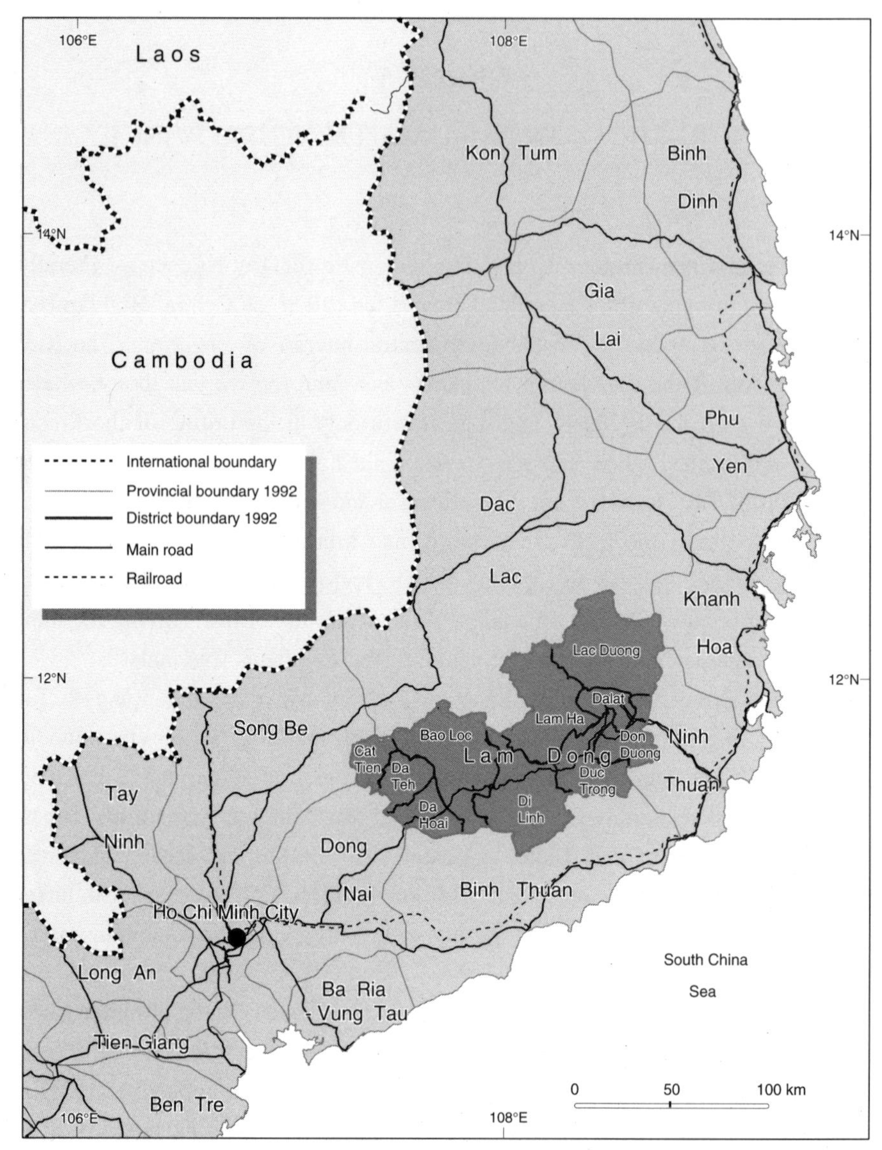

Production: Le défi forestier au Vietnam, 1996

Figure 13. Lam Dong province and its region since 1992.

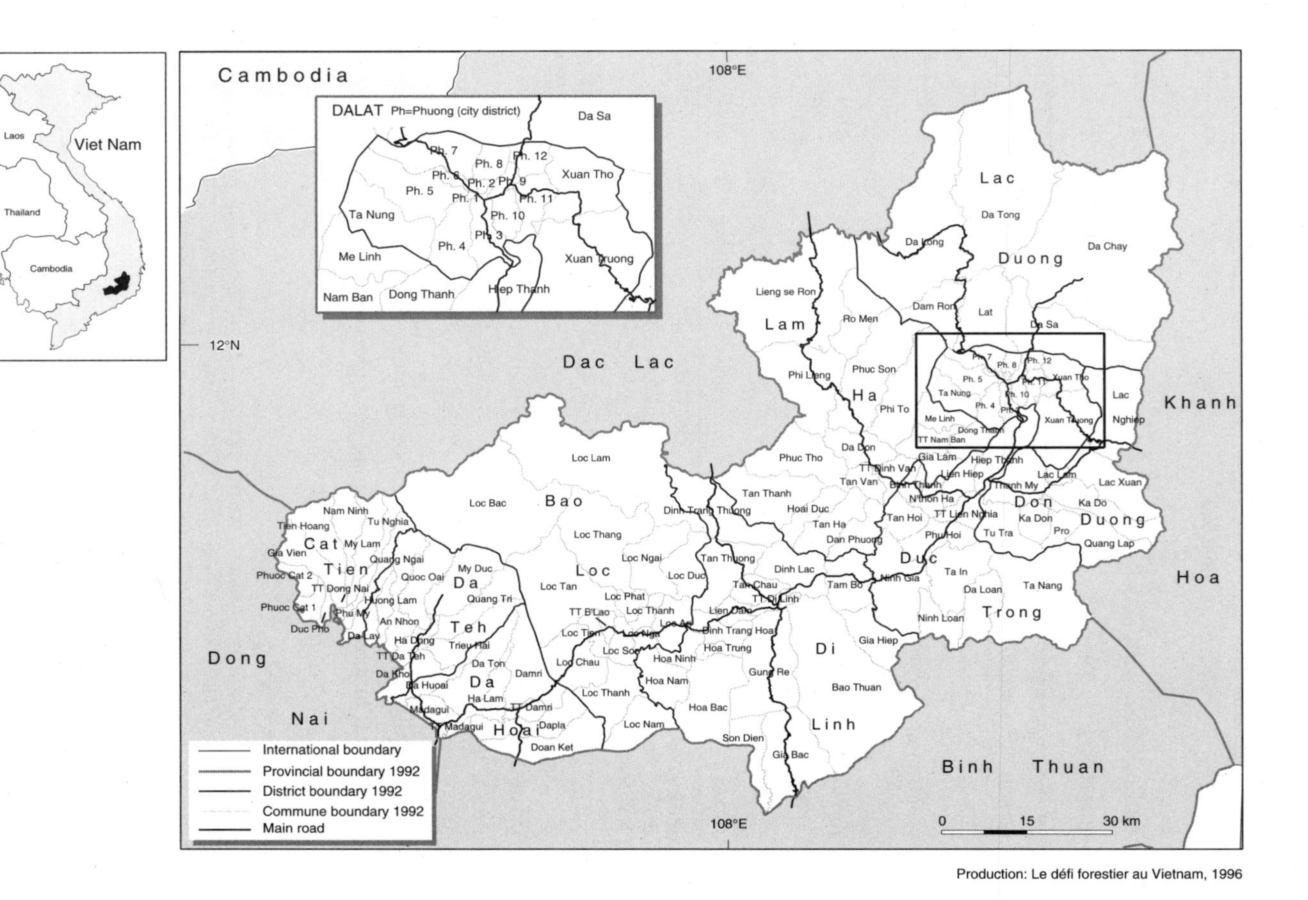

Figure 14. Lam Dong: administrative units, 1992. Source: Entreprise de cartographie, Dalat, 1982.

Table 9. Lam Dong province: changes in ethnic composition of the population, by group, 1976–89.

	1976		1979		1989	
	(*n*)	(%)	(*n*)	(%)	(*n*)	(%)
Kinh	223 332	65.2	269 989	69.5	488 462	76.4
Co Ho	56 520	16.5	63 678	16.4	82 971	13.0
Ma	19 009	5.6	15 910	4.1	19 792	3.1
Hoa	10 325	3.0	11 959	3.1	11 160	1.7
Tho	8 184	2.4	502	0.1	522	0.1
Churu	7 906	2.3	7 444	1.9	10 402	1.6
Nung	4 992	1.5	5 750	1.5	8 491	1.3
M'nong	4 687	1.4	4 164	1.1	4 285	0.7
Thai	3 181	0.9	2 887	0.7	3 731	0.6
Xtiêng	562	0.2	2	0.0	132	0.0
Kho Me	380	0.1	315	0.1	397	0.1
Tay	224	0.1	4 479	1.2	6 605	1.0
Others [a]	3 141	0.9	1 177	0.3	2 339	0.3

Source: LDPSB (1981); Tran Si Thu (1992).
[a] Includes Bana, Cham, Choro, Co, Dao, Ede, Gia Rai, Giay, Gie Triêng, Hmong, H'Re, Muong, Rag Rai, San Chay, San Diu, and a few unidentified groups.

surpassed 870 000 inhabitants.[28] Like Tuyen Quang province, Lam Dong is home to a rich cultural heritage: its population comprises, besides the Kinh, some 25 ethnic minorities (Table 9).

The topography of Lam Dong province is more complex than that of Tuyen Quang, as it has higher, steeper, and more entangled landforms (Figure 16).

[28]Statistical data, notably those dealing with demographic characteristics, are particularly difficult to collect, process, and map out in the case of Lam Dong province. Among the reasons for these difficulties is the administrative history of Lam Dong, whose current boundaries are fairly recent. In fact, the very name Lam Dong is the result of a geographical and toponymical compromise, having components drawn from the names of two former provinces: the *Lam* comes from Lam Vien, a Vietnamized version of a local name (Lang Biang), and the *Dong* comes from Dong Nai Thuong, which means "Upper Dong Nai" (the Dong Nai River forms the major physiographic axis of the province). The province of Upper Dong Nai (the *Haut Dong Nai* of the French colonial administration) was established in 1899, and its boundaries have since been modified several times. The province of Lam Dong was established in 1958 from a regrouping of several preexisting districts and provinces, but its current boundaries were drawn in early 1976 (De Koninck 1996). In addition, since then several changes have been made, within the province itself, to the various district boundaries and, even more so, to the boundaries of the communes, whose names and numbers have been modified on numerous occasions (Figure 15). Given these problems and obstacles, any diachronic mapping is a genuine feat.

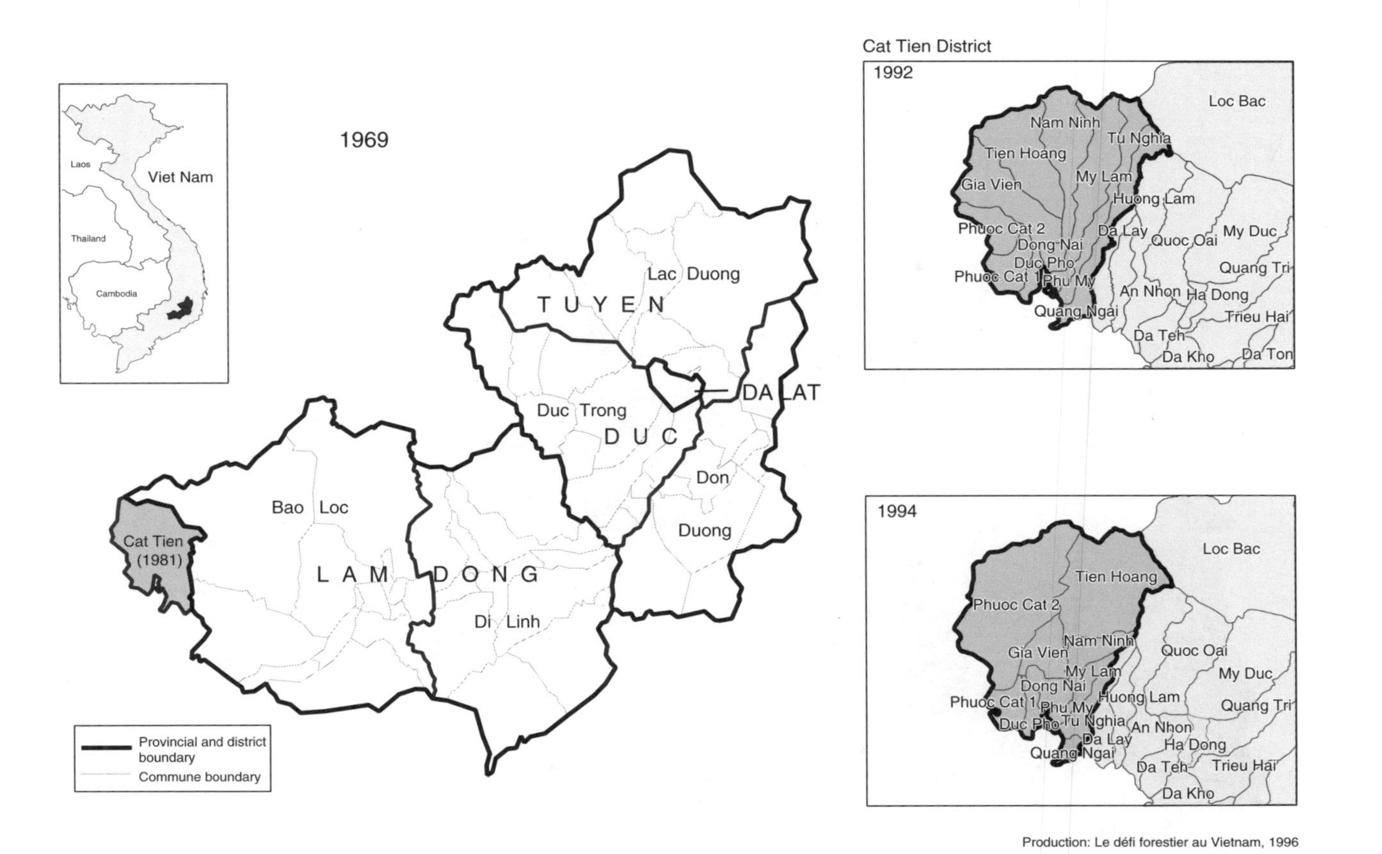

Figure 15. Lam Dong: examples of changes in commune boundaries, 1969–94. Source: Army Map Service, US Army Corps of Engineers, 1969; Entreprise de cartographie, Dalat, 1992.

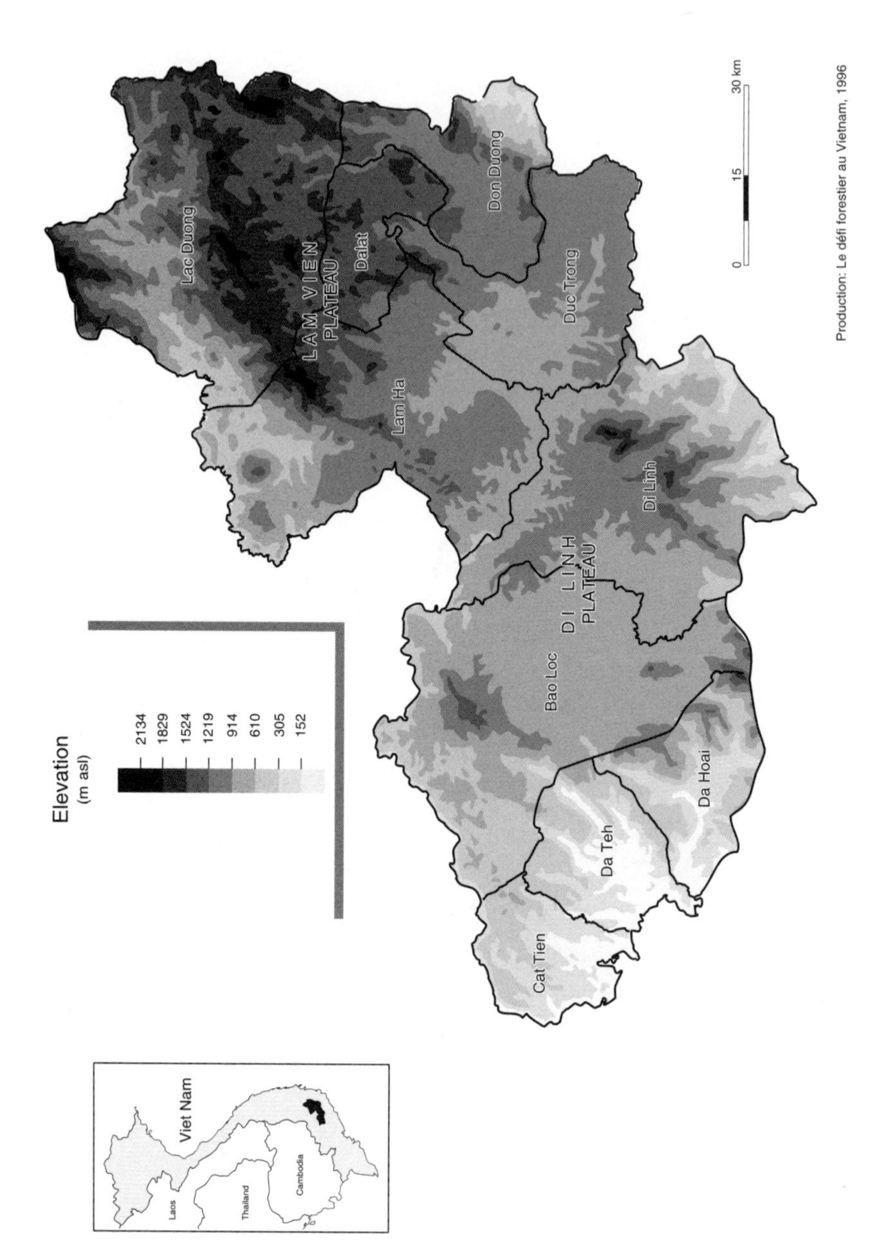

Figure 16. Lam Dong: landforms. Source: ESRI (1992).

From the southwest to the northeast, three landform levels can be identified. At the first, which encompasses the three small districts of Cat Tien, Da Teh, and Da Hoai, the altitude rises eastward from less than 150 m asl to more than 600 m asl, with some narrow ridges emerging above that altitude in the vicinity of the second level, or platform. This second level is more uniform, with an altitude averaging around 1 000 m asl. It corresponds to the Di Linh Plateau, which includes Di Linh district, Bao Loc district, and the westernmost sections of Duc Trong district. The heart of the plateau is covered with basaltic soils, which are particularly favourable to floristic biodiversity, as well as to commercial tree or bushy crops, such as coffee, tea, and mulberry (Figure 17).

These types of soils are also prevalent in the three small western districts, particularly in Cat Tien. Although they are also present in the more elevated (third-level) eastern districts — those that make up the Lam Vien Plateau — their overall share decreases to only a residual amount in the large district of Lac Duong. In addition, this third and highest level is more uniformly mountainous, with steeper slopes. The average altitude is about 1 500 m asl, with some ridges reaching beyond 2 000 m asl. The highest of these, situated in the largely mountainous district of Lac Duong, stands at some 2 400 m asl.

As a whole, Lam Dong province receives more rainfall than Tuyen Quang. The average annual total generally surpasses 2 000 mm, with, however, considerable local variation. The western portion of the province receives on average more than 3 600 mm/year, whereas in the eastern districts of Duc Trong and Don Duong, the average does not reach much beyond 2 000 mm/year, and it is even less than 1 600 mm/year over much of these two districts (Figure 18). In addition, seasonal concentration is very intense, with 80–90% of the annual total falling during the rainy season, between April and November.

Such abundant precipitation, falling on these tropical uplands with their irregular landforms and areas of fertile soils, contributes to the exceptional biodiversity, particularly noticeable in terms of plant species. These are dispersed among the montane forests, which are of several types, including the great pine forest (Figure 19).

Changes in land use

We were able to gain access to more abundant and better land-use data for this province than for Tuyen Quang. Notwithstanding the problem caused by the changes in the province's boundaries in late 1975, it was still possible to complete a more systematic diachronic mapping of the changes in land use. We ended up

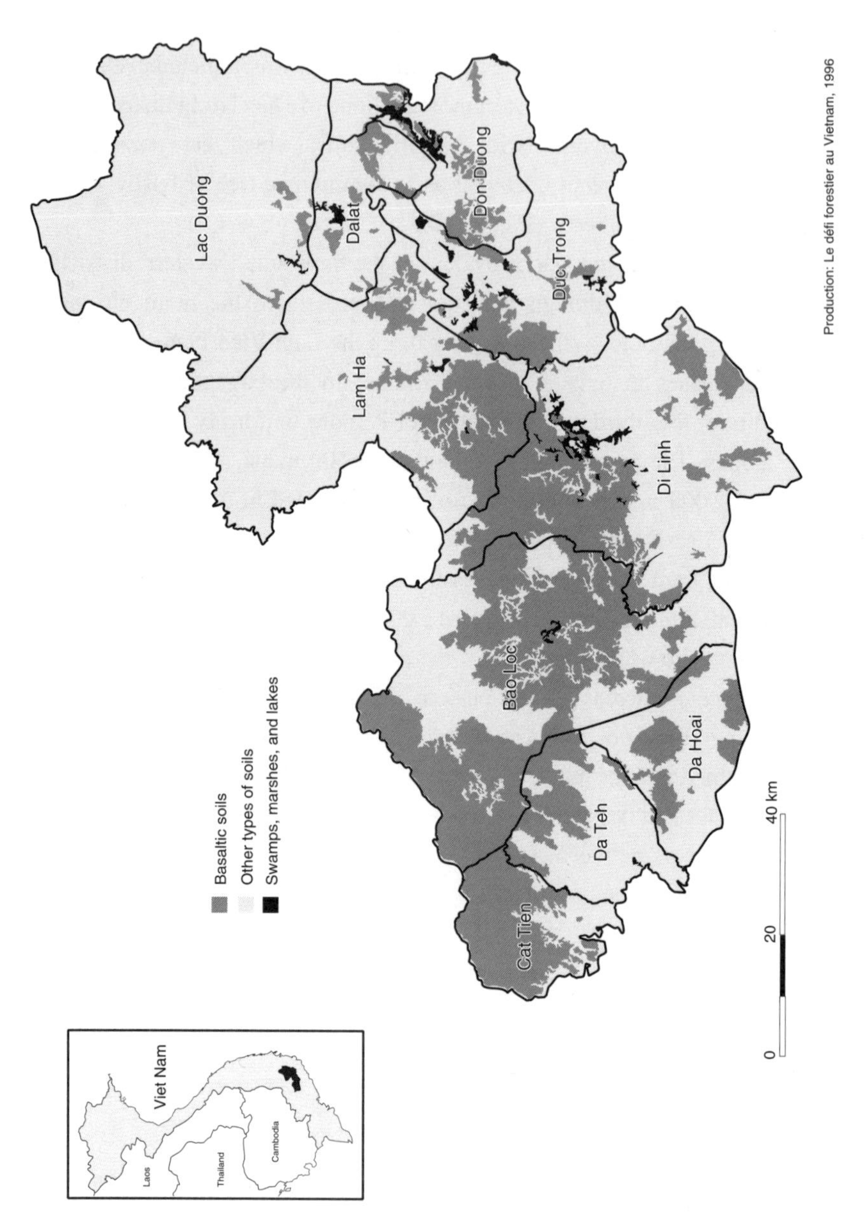

Figure 17. Lam Dong: major soil types. Source: Institut de planification des projets agricoles, Ho Chi Minh City, 1983.

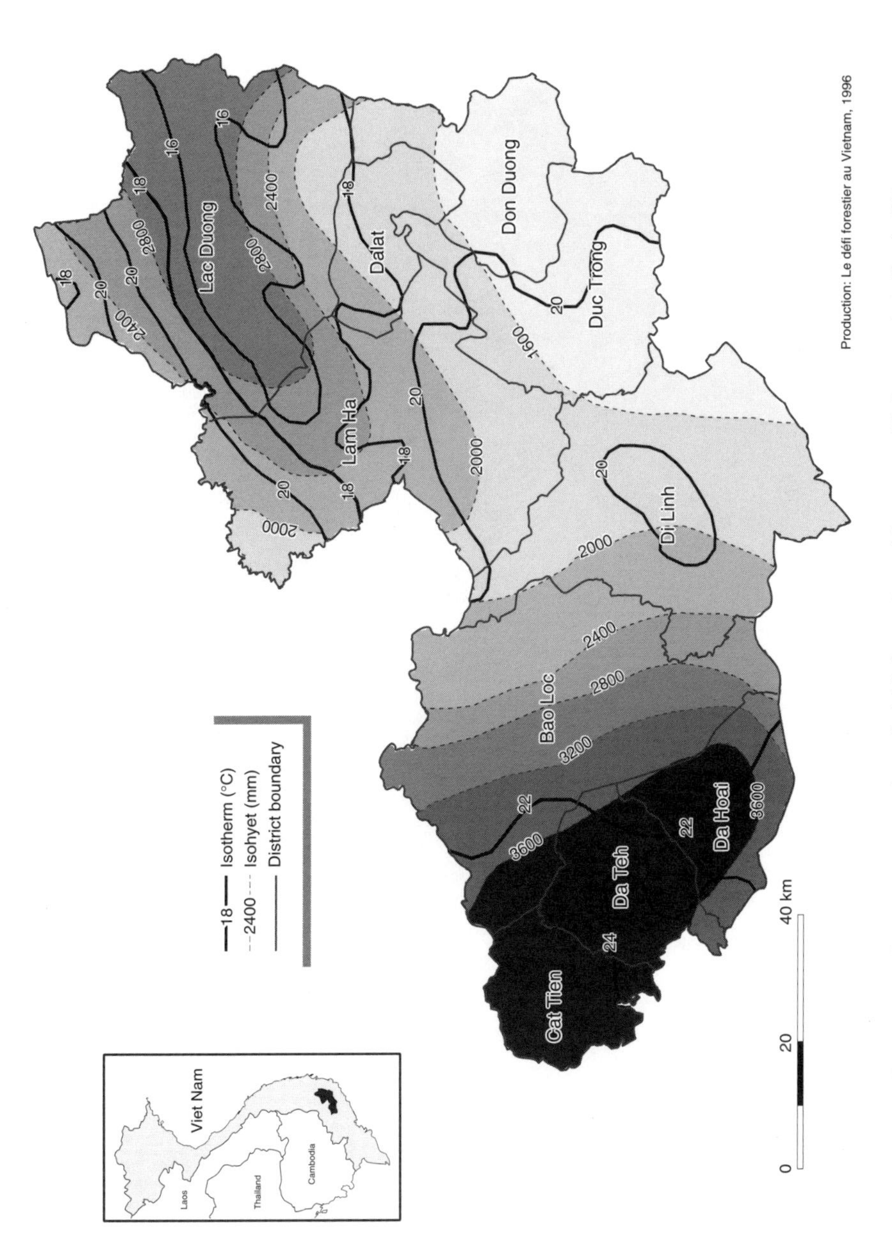

Figure 18. Lam Dong: temperature and annual rainfall. Source: General Department of Hydrometeorology, Hanoi, 1985.

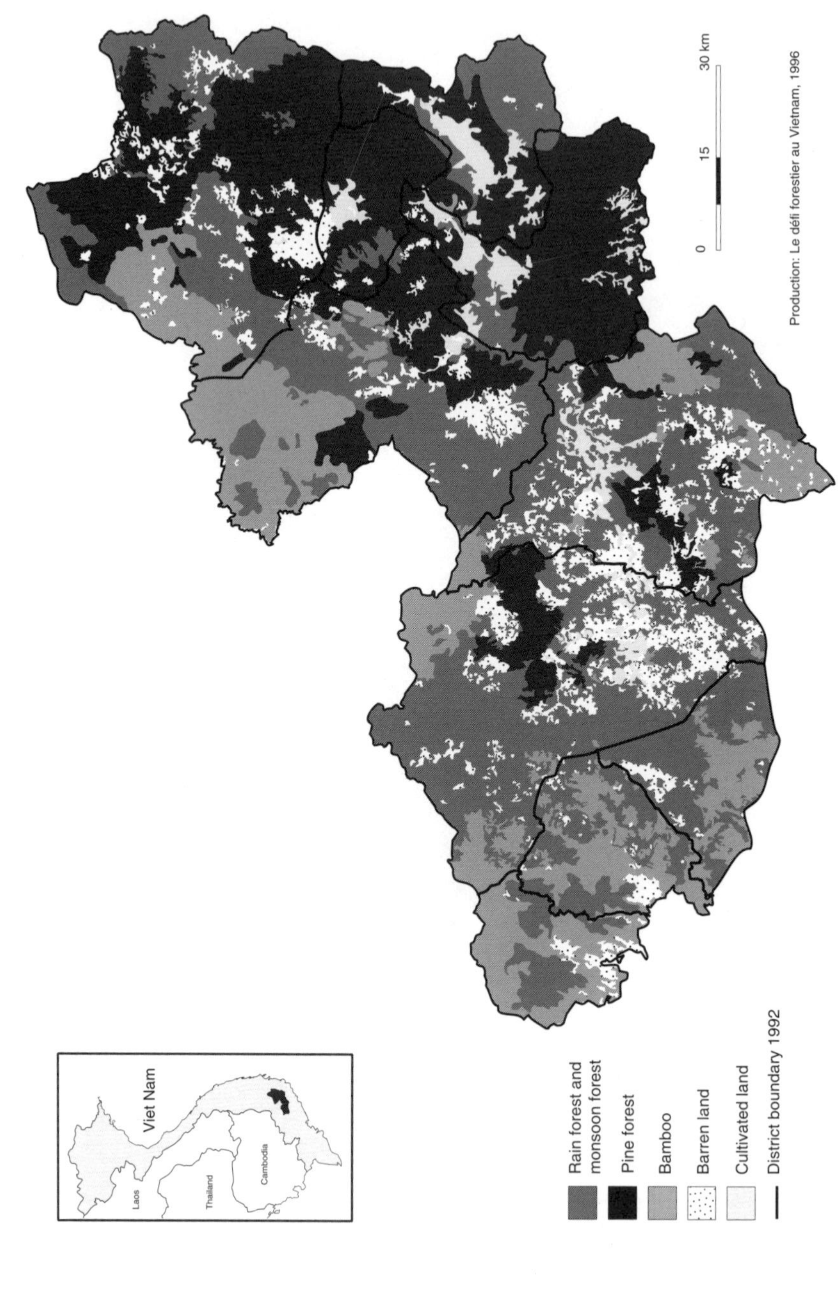

Figure 19. Lam Dong: land use, 1958. Source: Forest Inventory and Planning Institute, Hanoi, 1987 (based on 1958 airphotos).

drafting three maps. Involving several hundred hours of work,[29] these maps illustrate land use in Lam Dong province in 1958, 1979, and 1992 (Figures 19–24).

To draft these maps, however, we had to reduce the number and standardize the content of the land-use categories, thereby curtailing somewhat the illustration of the richness of forest types.[30] Some subcategories or classes were sometimes more detailed from one particular set of sources for a particular date, but given the resulting lack of comparability, we had to do some regrouping, thereby restricting the precision of our cartographic syntheses. Nevertheless, for the purpose of meeting the initial and central objectives of our research project, namely, the analysis and interpretation of the presumed causes of deforestation, the broader categories we retained appeared adequate.

The 1958 land-use map

Airphotos show that in 1958, nearly 70% of the province was covered with forest (Table 10; see also Figure 19).[31] Within this proportion, the ratio of leafy forest (rain forest and monsoon forest) to pine forest was 4 : 3. Cultivated land occupied less than 3% of the territory, and barren lands accounted for as much as 8%. However, as clearly revealed by the map (Figure 19), these proportions varied considerably between the districts.

First, the three westernmost districts, also the lowest in altitude, had no pine forest whatsoever.[32] However, in the eastward direction, as the land rises, the proportion of pine forests increased to the point where they covered 50–70% of the territory of the four easternmost districts, which form the Lam Vien Plateau. Furthermore, within these pine forests, along with the eastward rise in elevation, the three-needle pine trees (*Pinus kesiya*) were increasingly apparent. Thus, on the Lam Vien Plateau, such trees appeared predominant, but at the central and middle

---

[29]The work was burdensome for several reasons, including the need to rely on a very large number of land-use categories and the attempt we initially made to retain most of them. The digitization — to which several participants were being initiated — of this very detailed information became a monumental and costly task in terms of work time and material resources.

[30]These forest types, as represented on the source maps (which were based on airphoto interpretation), were quite numerous.

[31]All figures assembled in Table 10 were computed by planimetry from Figures 19–21.

[32]This description of the 1958 land-use map refers to districts as they have been known since 1987. For example, in 1958, the so-called western districts did not exist, that is, not under their current names, Cat Tien, Da Teh, and Da Hoai.

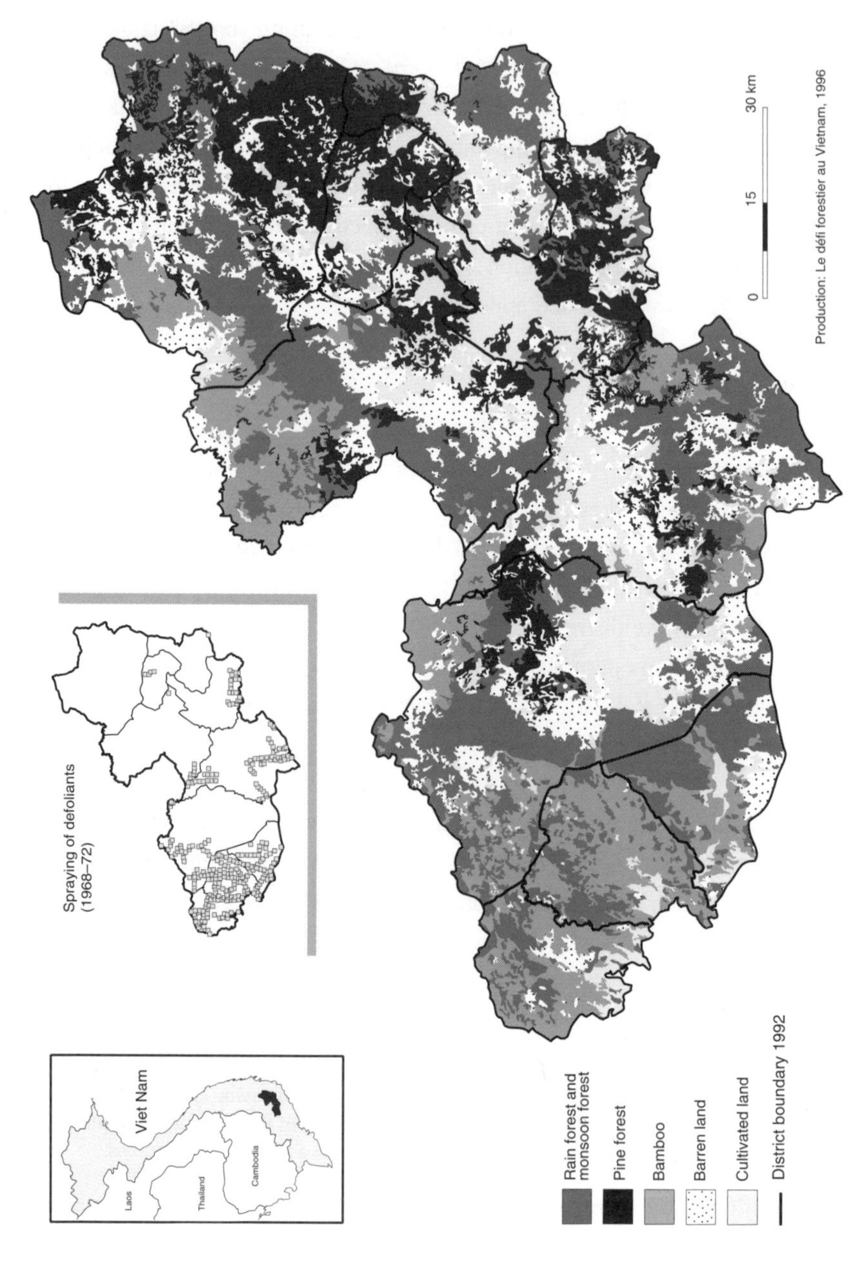

Figure 20. Lam Dong: land use, 1979. Source: Forest Inventory and Planning Institute, Hanoi, 1987.

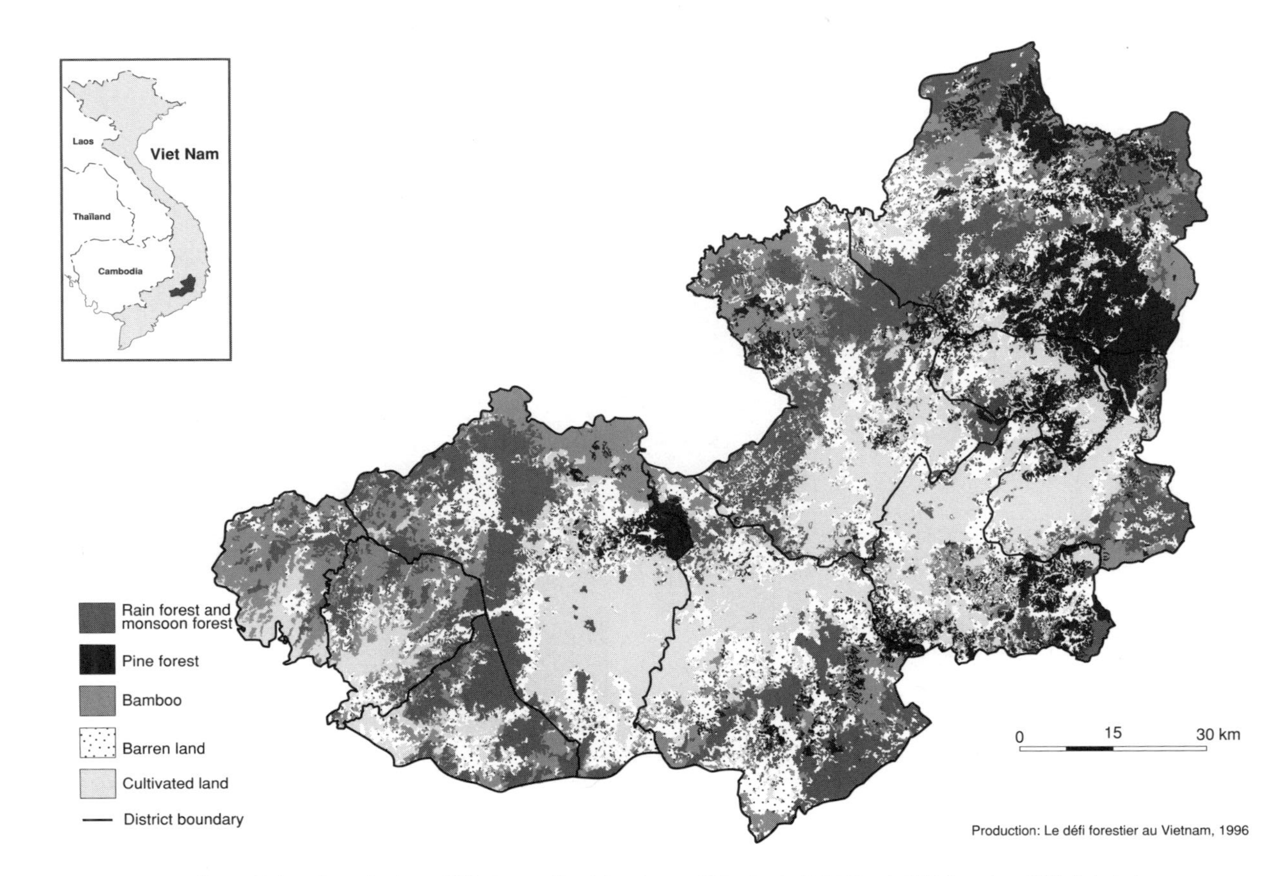

Figure 21. Lam Dong: land use, 1992. Source: Forest Inventory and Planning Institute, Hanoi, 1987 (based on 1992 airphotos).

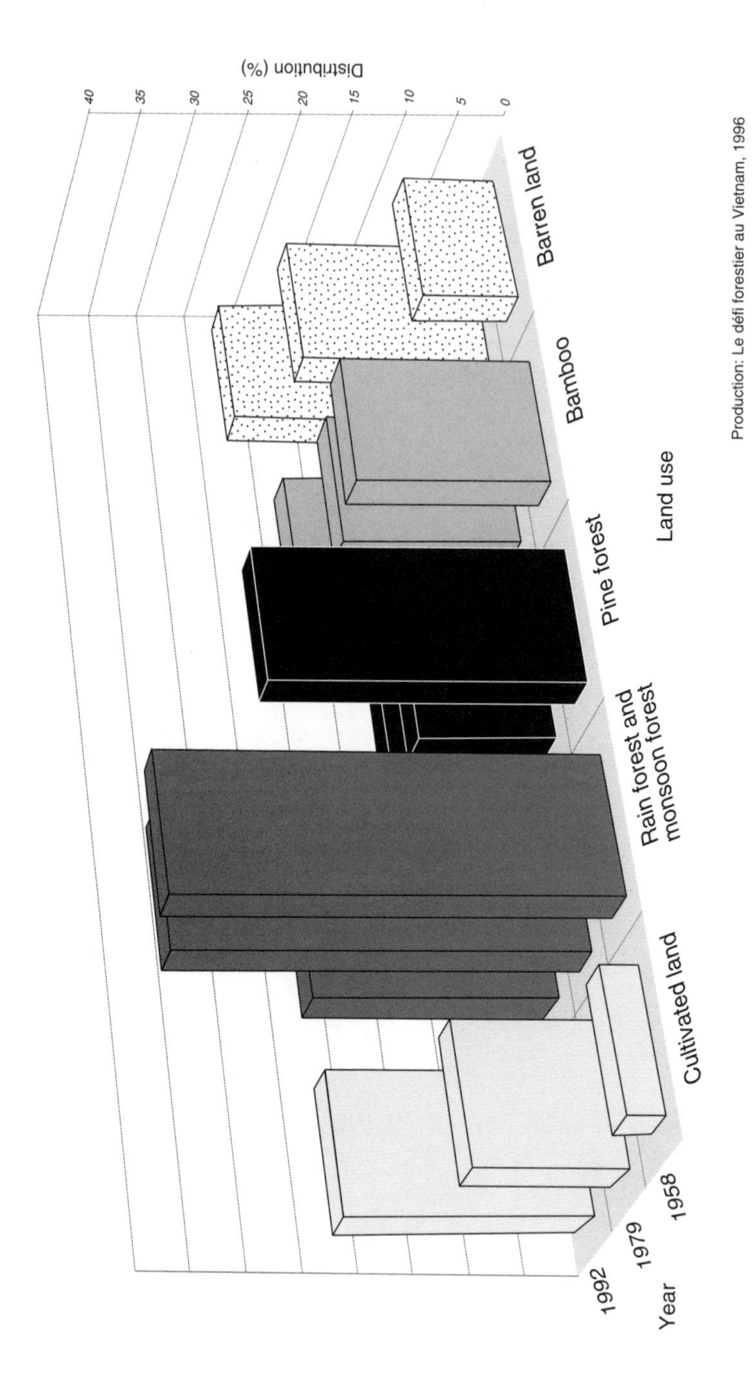

Figure 22. Lam Dong: changes in land use, 1958–92. Source: Forest Inventory and Planning Institute, Hanoi.

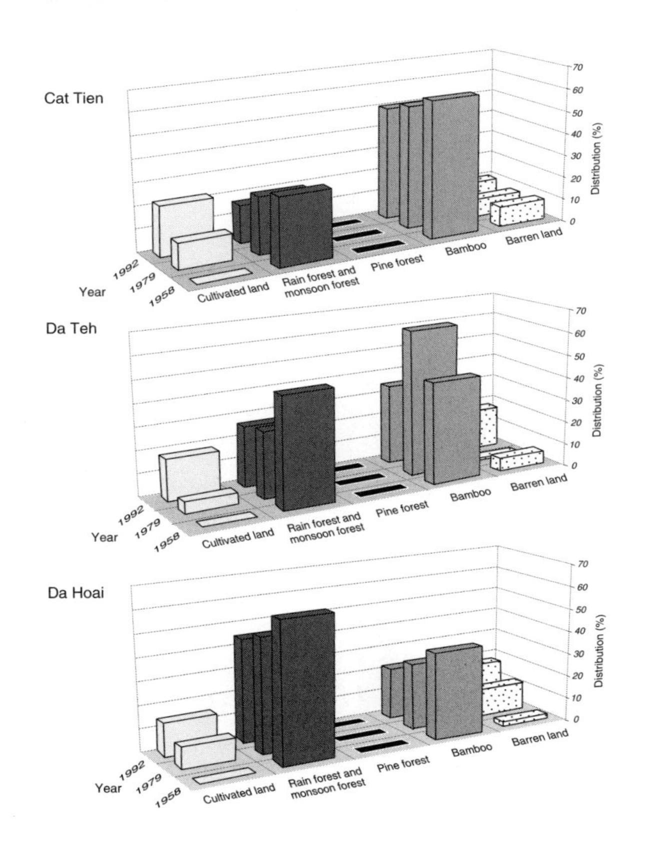

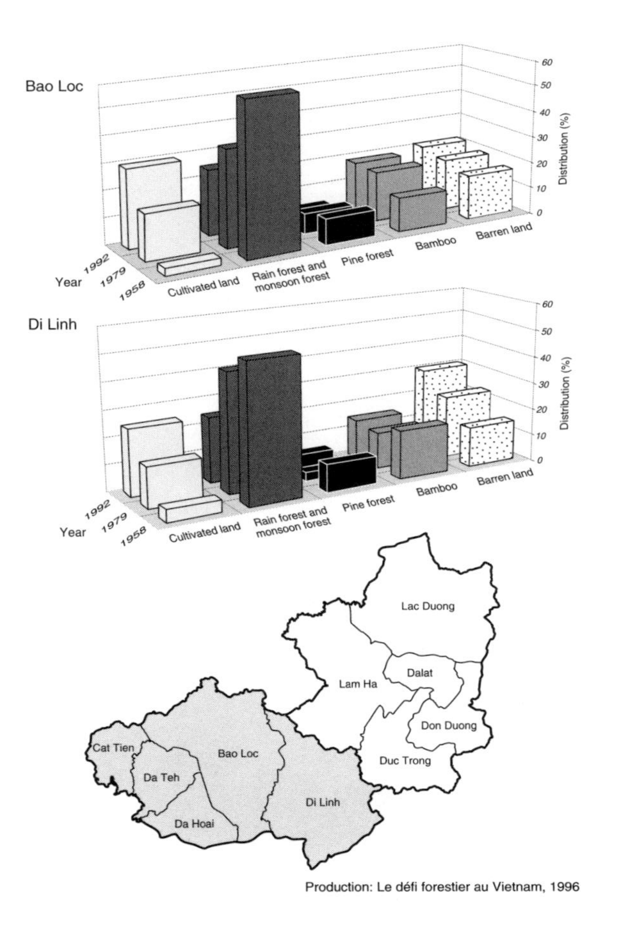

Figure 23. Lam Dong: changes in land use, Cat Tien, Da Teh, Da Hoai, Bao Loc, and Di Linh districts, 1958–92. Source: Forest Inventory and Planning Institute, Hanoi.

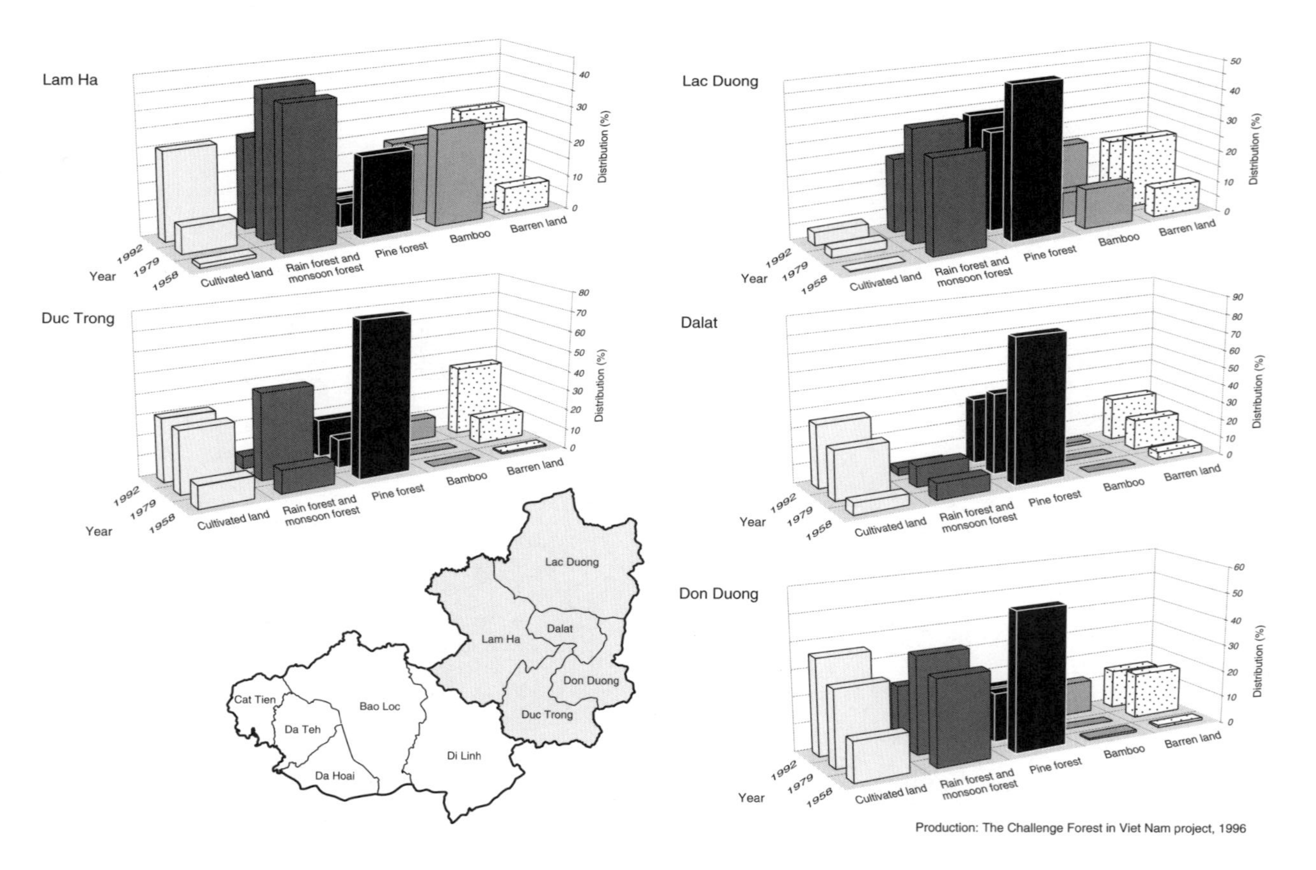

Figure 24. Lam Dong: changes in land use, Lam Ha, Duc Truong, Don Duong, Dalat, and Lac Duong districts, 1958–92. Source: Forest Inventory and Planning Institute, Hanoi.

levels, particularly in Bao Loc, Di Linh, and Lam Ha districts, the two-needle pine trees (*Pinus merkhusii*) competed with them for predominance.[33]

Second (and this point is a corollary), leafy forests predominated in areas of lower elevation and, hence, mostly in the western part of the province, although they were still very much present in the central districts at altitudes of more than 600 m asl, and even up to 900 m asl (see Figures 16 and 19). In these forests, dipterocarpaceous trees were widespread.

Third, bamboo forests — a degraded or at least intermediate formation within the forest cycle — covered nearly one-fifth of the province but with marked regional variation.[34] Bamboo forests, almost entirely absent from the eastern districts of Duc Trong and Don Duong, predominated in the three small western districts, covering more than 60% of Cat Tien (see Table 10).

Fourth, cultivated fields, to which as little as 3.5% of the territory was devoted, were essentially confined to a central discontinuous corridor that extended through Bao Loc, Di Linh, Duc Trong, and Don Duong districts, along national route 20. Such fields were totally absent from the three small western districts and hardly noticeable in the eastern mountainous district of Lac Duong, which was mostly inhabited by ethnic minorities.

Fifth, barren lands, which accounted for 9% of the total land use, also appeared to be unevenly distributed. Although they were largely represented in the central districts of Di Linh and, even more so, Bao Loc (17%), they were quite sparse in Don Duong and Duc Truong districts (less than 1%). However, in the very mountainous district of Lac Duong, barren lands accounted for a surprising 9% of land use, a figure that corresponds to the provincial average. Could this have been the result of excessive slash-and-burn practices, which at that time could only have been those of ethnic minorities? Or was this simply the beginning of a fallow period for lands that representatives of these minorities had put under cultivation for 1 or 2 years after clearing the land by fire?

---

[33]Although not represented on the map published here (Figure 19), these variations in the distribution of the two basic types of pine forests were quite evident on the airphotos we used to construct the map.

[34]It should be pointed out that throughout our study, as our tables and maps testify, we made it a point to distinguish between bamboo-covered areas and areas under other types of tree cover. We considered so-called bamboo forests to be a degraded form of forests but recognized that they may also represent a stage in the reconstitution of climax forests. In either case, our figures concerning the actual extent of forest cover are both uncompromising and distinct from those produced by generous or conciliatory observers who consider — wrongly, according to us — a bamboo forest to be a genuine, complete, and closed forest.

Table 10. Lam Dong province: changes in land use, by district, 1958–92.

	Cultivated land [a]		Rain and monsoon forests		Pine forest		Bamboo		Barren land	
	(km^2)	(%)	(km^2)	(%)	(km^2)	(%)	(km^2)	(%)	(km^2)	(%)
					1958					
Bao Loc	49	2.7	1 029	57.3	182	10.1	232	12.9	305	16.0
Cat Tien	0	0	124	29.9	0	0	253	61.0	38	9.2
Da Hoai	0	0	306	60.6	0	0	189	37.4	10	2.0
Dalat [b]	25	6.3	36	9.0	319	80.2	0	0	18	4.5
Da Teh	0	0	248	49.1	0	0	227	45.0	30	5.9
Di Linh	74	4.7	814	51.6	166	10.5	287	18.2	235	14.9
Don Duong	89	14.5	196	31.9	320	52.1	4	0.7	5	0.8
Duc Trong	97	11.0	99	11.2	676	76.7	2	0.2	7	0.8
Lac Duong	1	0.1	559	29.8	907	48.3	237	12.6	174	9.3
Lam Ha	18	1.1	637	40.1	368	23.2	439	27.7	125	7.9
Province	363	3.5	4 048	39.9	2 938	28.9	1 870	18.4	947	9.3

					1979					
Bao Loc	319	17.8	650	36.2	140	7.8	342	19.0	346	19.3
Cat Tien	48	11.6	105	25.3	0	0	228	54.9	34	8.2
Da Hoai	50	9.9	250	49.6	0	0	143	28.4	61	12.1
Dalat [b]	109	27.4	47	11.8	176	44.2	0	0	66	16.6
Da Teh	26	5.1	149	29.5	0	0	325	64.4	5	1.0
Di Linh	242	15.4	704	44.7	50	3.2	216	13.7	364	23.1
Don Duong	176	28.7	222	36.2	112	18.2	0	0	104	16.9
Duc Trong	270	30.6	376	42.6	122	13.8	0	0	114	12.9
Lac Duong	52	2.8	667	35.5	585	31.1	155	8.2	420	22.4
Lam Ha	120	7.6	667	42.0	111	7.0	328	20.7	362	22.8
Province	1 412	13.9	3 837	37.8	1 296	12.8	1 737	17.1	1 876	18.5

(continued)

Table 10 concluded.

	Cultivated land [a]		Rain and monsoon forests		Pine forest		Bamboo		Barren land	
	(km^2)	(%)	(km^2)	(%)	(km^2)	(%)	(km^2)	(%)	(km^2)	(%)
1992										
Bao Loc	537	29.9	451	25.1	78	4.3	344	19.1	387	21.5
Cat Tien	93	22.4	71	17.1	0	0	210	50.5	42	10.1
Da Hoai	75	14.9	226	44.9	0	0	112	22.3	90	17.9
Dalat [b]	138	34.8	17	4.3	142	35.8	7	1.8	93	23.4
Da Teh	94	18.5	139	27.4	0	0	181	35.7	93	18.3
Di Linh	392	24.9	389	24.7	82	5.2	233	14.8	479	30.4
Don Duong	221	35.9	131	21.3	97	15.8	76	12.4	90	14.6
Duc Trong	271	30.7	54	6.1	160	18.1	92	10.4	305	34.6
Lac Duong	78	4.1	438	23.3	633	33.7	377	20.0	355	18.9
Lam Ha	402	25.3	411	25.8	81	5.1	294	18.5	402	25.3
Province	2 301	22.6	2 327	22.9	1 273	12.5	1 926	19.0	2 336	23.0

Source: Figures 19–21.
[a] To facilitate interannual comparison, this category was defined to include settlements.
[b] Township.

The 1979 land-use map

Comparing the land-use map of 1979 with that of 1958 allowed us to identify a number of drastic changes (see Figures 19 and 20 and Table 10). First, it seems that the entire forest cover had been taken to task. However, the considerable loss of forest cover, reduced from 69% to 51% of total land use, was essentially accounted for by the retreat of pine forests, as the other types of forests lost little ground.[35] Although the pine forest's share of total land use receded from 29% to 13%, the rain and monsoon forests accounted for 38% in 1979, compared to 40% in 1958. What had happened?

Second, a very substantial expansion of agricultural land occurred in the heart of the province at the second level, on the Di Linh Plateau, as well as on the fringe of the third level, on the Lam Vien Plateau. In other words, the central agricultural corridor was considerably widened. Thus, in Bao Loc, Di Linh, and Dalat districts, the share of cultivated land grew from 2.7% to 17.8%, from 4.7% to 15.4%, and from 6.3% to 27.4%, respectively. In Lam Ha district, which in 1958 appeared only marginally opened to sedentary forms of agriculture, the proportion of land devoted to permanently cultivated fields went from 1.1% to 7.6%, whereas in the eastern districts of Duc Trong and Don Duong, agricultural expansion, although less considerable in terms of total area covered, was still significant in proportionate terms (see Table 10). Even the western part of the province was involved in this agricultural expansion, as the small districts of Cat Tien, Da Teh, and Da Hoai, until then totally deprived of permanently cultivated fields, saw their agricultural acumen begin to take form. Overall, for the whole province, the proportion of cultivated land grew from 3.5% to 13.9%. Only the easternmost district of Lac Duong, which was mountainous and difficult to access, appeared to be relatively uninvolved in this dynamic expansion.

Third, however, in Lac Duong, as well as in several other districts, the extent of barren lands increased dramatically; for the province as a whole, the barren lands increased from 9.3% to 18.3% of total land area. The spread of barren lands was noticeable in every district, with the exception of Bao Loc and Cat Tien, where they lost some ground. The origin of these barren lands is not easily traceable or deducible, even from a comparison of their distribution as illustrated on the two land-use maps. In place of some cultivated fields represented on the 1958 map, some patches of barren land appear on the 1979 map. In addition, some expanses of forest were replaced by barren lands (see Figures 19 and 20). In the first case, we may be dealing with fields abandoned for reasons of soil degradation or

[35]The distinction established here (Figures 19 and 20 and Table 10) between rain forests and monsoon forests, on the one hand, and pine forests, on the other, is essentially operational, because the pine forests actually belong to the world of montane rain forests (Whitmore 1990).

exhaustion; in the second, we may be seeing cases of forest lands that had been cleared and put under cultivation after 1958 but abandoned before 1979. In the latter case, one can speculate that "professional" swiddening by representatives of ethnic minorities was responsible, as well as "amateur" swiddening of the type practiced by Kinh colonists. These people seemed to have been intent on definitely clearing the forest so that they could devote the land to perennial cultivation, at least until the recently cleared land parcels were exhausted, particularly those along steep slopes, where eventually more forest would be cut down to again make way for crops. These hypotheses could probably be verified through case studies involving careful groundwork, as well as detailed sociohistorical surveys. Such initiatives were in fact partially taken during the project.

Fourth, in any case, attempts to analyze the cycle followed by bamboo forests should also be made at a more local scale, as the pattern of change revealed by a comparison of their distribution at the scale of the whole province in 1958 and 1979 is not easily decoded. Overall, the extent of bamboo forests was barely reduced (from 18.4% to 17.1%), although the changes at the district level were not obviously uniform. In some districts, such as Bao Loc and Da Teh, bamboo forests gained some ground, but in others — such as Cat Tien, Da Hoai, Lam Ha, and Lac Duong — they lost at least as much. In some areas, such as in southern Da Hoai and in western Lac Duong, some bamboo forests gave way to cultivated fields; in others, for example, again in southern Da Hoai and in northern Lam Ha, they were decimated, giving way to barren lands. In some rarer and smaller locations, such as in northwestern Cat Tien, bamboo forests were starting to achieve the status of large forests (rain forests or monsoon forests).

The 1992 land-use map

The 1992 land-use map (see Figure 21) is based on more abundant and more reliable information and thus is more accurate. It underlines and confirms, with increasing precision, the nature of the land-use changes already revealed by the comparison of the 1958 and 1979 maps.

First, the 1992 land-use map illustrates clearly the continued expansion of cultivated lands, following an even more rapid average annual rhythm, as revealed by planimetric computations (see Table 10). Whereas over the 21 years separating the 1958 and 1979 surveys the share of cultivated land increased from 3.5% to 13.9%, between 1979 and 1992 (hence, over 13 years) it progressed to 22.6%.

Second, the 1992 map shows that the retreat of large forests (excluding bamboo forests) had continued; their share of total land use receded from 50.6% to 35.4%. However, in this instance, the so-called rain and monsoon forests, essentially found at the lower altitudes, were taken to task. The large pine forests lost very little ground; their share of total land use only decreased from 12.8% to 12.5% between 1979 and 1992. It does seem that the pine forests benefited from a respite, probably thanks to better enforcement of protection policies, whereas the other types of large forest formations were exposed to a real massacre; over 13 years, their share of total land use dropped from 37.8% to 22.9% (see Table 10). In absolute figures, the loss of these types of forest formations reached some 150 000 ha (from 380 000 ha to 230 000 ha), an average loss of more than 11 500 ha per year. Considering that cultivated lands increased by some 90 000 ha during the same period, one must conclude that forests gave way not only to agriculture but also to other forms of land use.

Third, bamboo forests, in fact, gained a little bit of ground (nearly 2%) during the same period (1979–92), following a pattern of change somewhat reminiscent of the one that prevailed during the preceding period (1958–79).

Fourth, the spread of barren lands was, however, proportionately, as well as absolutely, much more significant. Since 1979 barrenness had expanded over an additional 46 000 ha, accounting for 23% of total provincial land use by 1992 (about the same as agriculture, 22.6%).[36] Overall, it appears quite evident that between 1979 and 1992, more than 60% of the former territory of the cleared forests was taken over by cultivated fields tended by sedentary peasants, essentially belonging to the Kinh group; and more than about 30%, by barren lands. The rest of the cleared forests gave way, at least partly, to degraded forms of forest formations, including bamboo.

Everything considered, the two most striking changes in the landscape were the retreat of the forest and agricultural expansion. The latter followed a standard pattern, namely, a gradual and systematic enlargement, both of the central corridor and of the nuclei that had been formed during the preceding period in the three small western districts. But the detailed distribution of cultivated fields and barren lands, which often appear juxtaposed, reveals that this expansion seems to have taken an increasingly anarchic form. The local extension of both types of lands, cultivated and barren, was pursued in all directions, with frequent penetrations deep into the last remaining forested areas, as well as over most of the regions that make up the three small western districts and, finally, in northern Lam Ha and northern Lac Duong.

---

[36]However impressive, that figure of 23% for the share of barren lands in total provincial land use is significantly lower than that for Tuyen Quang province, which was 64.5% in 1992 (see Table 5).

Changes in the population and its distribution

The changes in the population of the territory that today constitutes Lam Dong province are not easily reconstructed. As pointed out above, the province was only established within its current boundaries in early 1976, and the boundaries of the various districts and a large number of the communes of the province have since been modified several times.

Immediately following the 1975/76 reunification of the country, the NEZs, many of which had been opened in northern Viet Nam during the 1960s, were extended into the Central Plateaus and particularly into Lam Dong province. This was followed by massive migrations of pioneer settlers, planned and monitored, at least officially, by the Vietnamese state, which was obviously pursuing several concurrent objectives. The major objectives were to provide a demographic safety outlet for the congested lowland areas of the country; to foster the development of commercial agriculture orientated toward export markets; and to establish firmer mastery over a region and its inhabitants, which had in the past managed to largely elude the control of the central government (De Koninck 1996; De Koninck et al. 1996). The impact on the province's population was considerable: between 1979 and 1989 (two census years), the population increased from 388 244 to 639 224, a 65% jump (Table 11). This exceptional growth, the pace of which has apparently been maintained, involved all districts with nearly equivalent intensity, resulting in substantial increases in population densities across the province.

The expansion of Kinh settlement

Unfortunately, data that would allow us to calculate the changes in the proportion of Kinh in the population at the scale of individual districts were unavailable. However, we did gain access to figures allowing us to compute the changes in the province's ethnic composition from 1976 — the year that followed the establishment of modern Lam Dong — to 1979 and through to 1989 (see Table 9). According to these figures, the Kinh's share of the total provincial population increased from 65.2%, to 69.5%, and then to 76.4%.

The much more rapid rate of growth of this share during the 1976–79 period was probably due to the fact that the establishment and settlement of the NEZs were most intensive during the very first years that followed reunification.[37] Figures on the proportion of Kinh in the population of the various districts

[37]We were able to collect only very scant and incomplete information — whether historical, geographical, or statistical — concerning these NEZs.

Table 11. Lam Dong province: area, population, and population density, by district, 1979–89.

	Area (km^2)	Population, 1979		Population, 1989		
		(*n*)	(inhabitants/km^2)	(*n*)	(inhabitants/km^2)	Kinh (%)
Bao Loc	1 773	78 100	44	128 587	73	84.6
Cat Tien	359	15 751	44	25 933	72	94.7
Da Hoai	573	13 386	23	22 040	38	82.7
Dalat [a]	419	70 430	168	115 959	277	96.9
Da Teh	473	20 953	44	34 498	73	93.1
Di Linh	1 570	45 557	29	75 007	48	56.1
Don Duong	639	36 566	57	60 204	94	70.6
Duc Trong	897	60 465	67	99 552	111	64.2
Lac Duong	1 882	10 917	6	17 974	10	5.9
Lam Ha	1 588	36 119	23	59 470	37	72.5
Province	10 173	388 244	38	639 224	63	76.4

Source: National census.
[a] Township.

were only available from the 1989 census data (see Table 11).[38] It varied from more than 90% in Dalat, Cat Tien, and Da Teh districts (the latter two located in the western portion of the province) to about 6% in Lac Duong (at the eastern end). The Kinh's share was well below the 76.4% provincial average in two additional districts, Di Linh (56.1%) and Duc Trong (64.2%).

The overall result in terms of population distribution and density is a very evident double correlation: one relating higher densities with areas having a predominantly Kinh population; and the other relating lower densities with areas having a predominantly non-Kinh population (Figure 25). In other words, the higher the population density in any given commune, the more likely it is to be attributable to a higher proportion of Kinh among the population.

Finally, it must be noted that nearly every one of the minority communities lost ground, in proportional demographic terms, in relation to the Kinh. Furthermore, in some cases, such as in that of the Ma, absolute numbers barely increased, and in other cases they even dropped dramatically. For example, the Tho population in the province fell from 8 184 in 1976 to 522 in 1989 (see Table 9). Only one group, the Tay,[39] migrating down from the north, grew substantially, although the overall total remained modest: the number of Tay increased from 224 to 6 605, still barely 1% of Lam Dong's total population. Other groups, such as the Nung, nearly managed to maintain their proportionate demographic share, also possibly thanks to migrations from the northern provinces.

The continuing expansion of settlement

The fact that planned migrations of Kinh settlers probably reached their apex during the late 1970s cannot be confirmed by the 1979 and 1989 census figures. These do, however, reveal that these migrations were continuing. It seems that what the Vietnamese themselves call spontaneous migrations have remained quite substantial, somewhat like in Indonesia, where the migrations of "spontan" settlers are nearly as important as those of official transmigration settlers (De Koninck and Déry 1997). In Viet Nam and, possibly even more so, in Indonesia, the authorities

---

[38]It should be pointed out that several Vietnamese government or quasi-government agencies regularly put out updated demographic data. But these are almost always the results of across-the-board mathematical projections that do not take into account the various differences that exist among the districts and communes, especially in the Central Highland provinces. Published in so-called yearbooks, these figures are of some use when they pertain to the whole country and perhaps the provinces, but they are very dubious and must therefore be handled with utmost caution when they pertain to districts and communes.

[39]Some observers consider the Tho to be a Tay subgroup, one of the most Vietnamized.

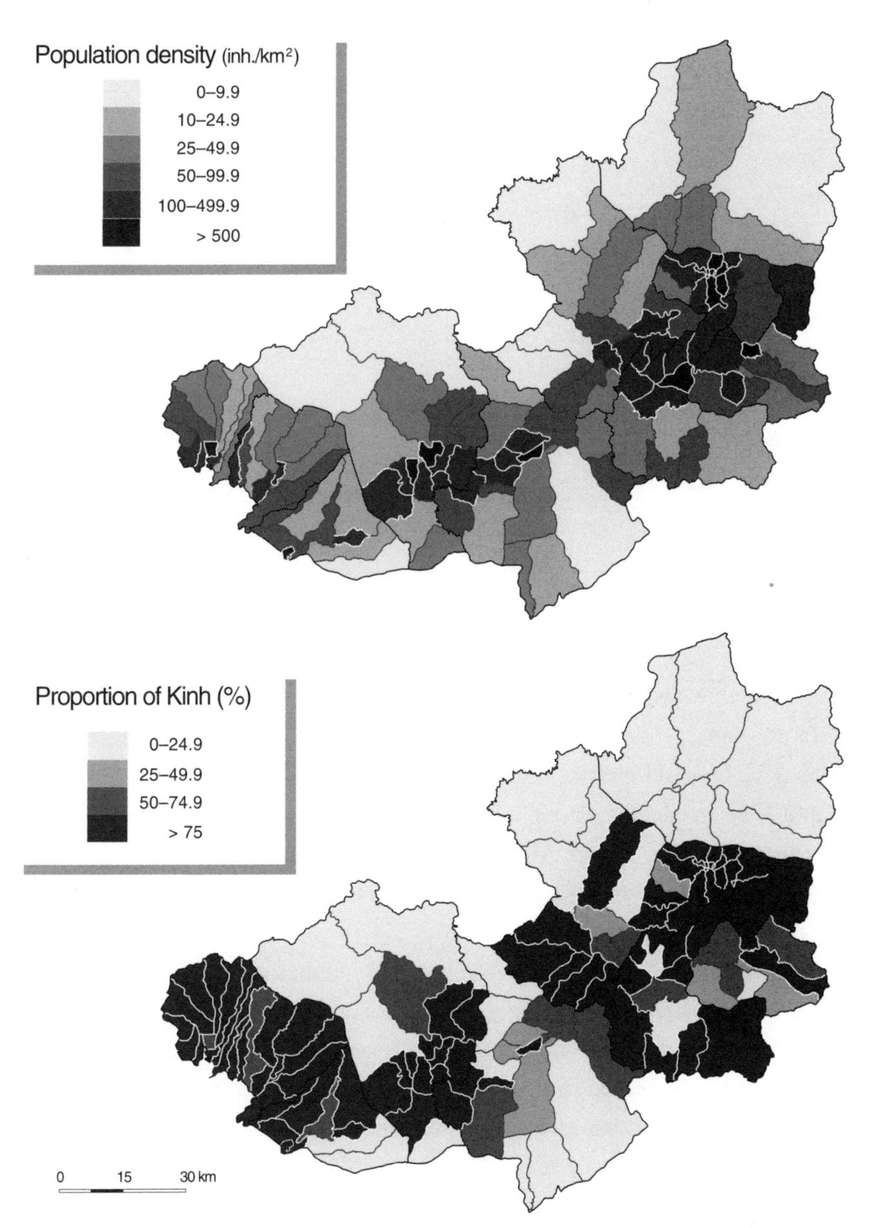

Figure 25. Lam Dong: population density and proportion of Kinh in the population, by commune, 1989. Source: Viet Nam Census Office, Hanoi (1989 census). Note: inh., inhabitants.

Table 12. Lam Dong province: spontaneous inmigrations, by district, 1987–93.

	Number of families having spontaneously migrated to Lam Dong						
	1987	1988	1989	1990	1991	1992	1993
Bao Loc	413	501	714	1 445	1 659	1 983	1 437
Cat Tien	176	214	305	617	796	897	329
Da Hoai	58	70	100	202	339	270	237
Dalat [a]	?	?	?	?	?	?	?
Da Teh	101	122	174	353	319	286	140
Di Linh	36	44	62	126	1 574	147	1 012
Don Duong	?	?	?	?	?	?	?
Duc Trong	0	0	0	0	376	448	632
Lac Duong	36	44	62	126	30	48	126
Lam Ha	225	272	388	785	680	764	1 002

Source: Data collected by Tran Dac Dan, University of Agriculture and Forestry, 1994.
[a] Township.

remain evasive regarding the overall numbers involved. Nevertheless, we were able to assemble some information on this topic (Table 12).[40] This seems to confirm the widespread but insufficiently documented fact that spontaneous migrations have been on the rise throughout Viet Nam. Such was the case between 1987 and 1993 in each of the eight districts of Lam Dong for which figures were obtained. In addition, thanks to frequent field trips carried out throughout the province, several members of our research team were able to witness the ongoing progress of the pioneer fronts.

In fact, if one looks more closely at the number of people involved, this renewed thrust toward Lam Dong seems quite substantial. During those 7 years (1987–93), 23 000 families of spontaneous, or independent, pioneers, or some 100 000 individuals, settled in this province whose population, in 1986, was still less than 600 000. Such inmigration figures seem quite plausible if one considers that between the two census years of 1979 and 1989, Lam Dong's population went from 388 244 to 639 224, a 65% increase over a 10-year period (see Table 11).

Some districts, in particular Bao Loc, Di Linh, and Lam Ha, appear to have been prime destinations for the incoming settlers, although the most noticeable impact seems to have been felt in the small district of Cat Tien, with an area only one-fifth that of Bao Loc. In fact, the increasing importance of the three small

[40]This information was collected by Tran Dac Dan, of the UAF, and presented during the final project workshop, held in Hanoi in May 1996.

western districts for pioneers, already revealed by the changes in land use (see Figures 19–21), is confirmed by another phenomenon: diachronic mapping of the gravity centre of the province's agriculture shows that it was moving westward (Figure 26). Such a mode of illustration has it limits, of course, as it does not account for the specific nature of the agricultural expansion. Furthermore, this specificity, the exact origin of the colonists, the routes that they followed to the highlands, and the timing and conditions of their actual settlement in their new environment are not sufficiently known.

Nevertheless, through our frequent field visits and the interviews and data collection we carried out among the population and with the local authorities in various localities of the Central Plateaus, we could identify, at least on a broad scale, some of the characteristics of the pioneering momentum. Thus, in a country where the land market has been experiencing a real boom, it seems that the so-called spontaneous migrations would be better described by the term *clandestine*. It does seem that the Central Highlands have continued to be a favoured destination for the representatives of ethnic minorities migrating down from the six northern provinces bordering on China (Cao Bang, Ha Giang, Lai Chau, Lang Son, Lao Cai, and Quang Ninh). Owing to severe environmental deterioration, caused at least partly by excessive farming on steep slopes, these provinces generate a lot of outmigration. As a result, Hmong and Tay–Nung families, after moving southward to the Central Plateaus, settle temporarily on the margins of the pioneer areas.[41] There, they take charge of cutting down the forest, and the cleared land is then made available for cultivation, for a fee, to Kinh colonists who have generally recently moved into the area from the lowlands of Annam or the Red River delta.[42] Such a division of labour often leads the authorities to lay the blame for the destruction of the forest solely on the ethnic minorities.

The agricultural frontier thus continues to expand rapidly at the expense of the forest, with the newly planted crops, such as coffee or cashew trees, generally being of the perennial type. Given both the pace at which the frontier is spreading and the reticence of the authorities to actually admit this and to recognize the nature of the alliances that fuel its overall progression — including the role of members of the armed forces, some of whom are actively involved on the

[41]A comparison of the 1979 and 1989 census figures does seem to confirm this migratory movement of the Nung, whose number in Lam Dong province increased from 5 750 to 8 491 (see Table 9).

[42]We were able to reconstruct this scenario in May 1995, on the occasion of a extended tour of several of the NEZs. It was verified further through additional field observations made in 1996, 1997, and 1998 by several members of the research team.

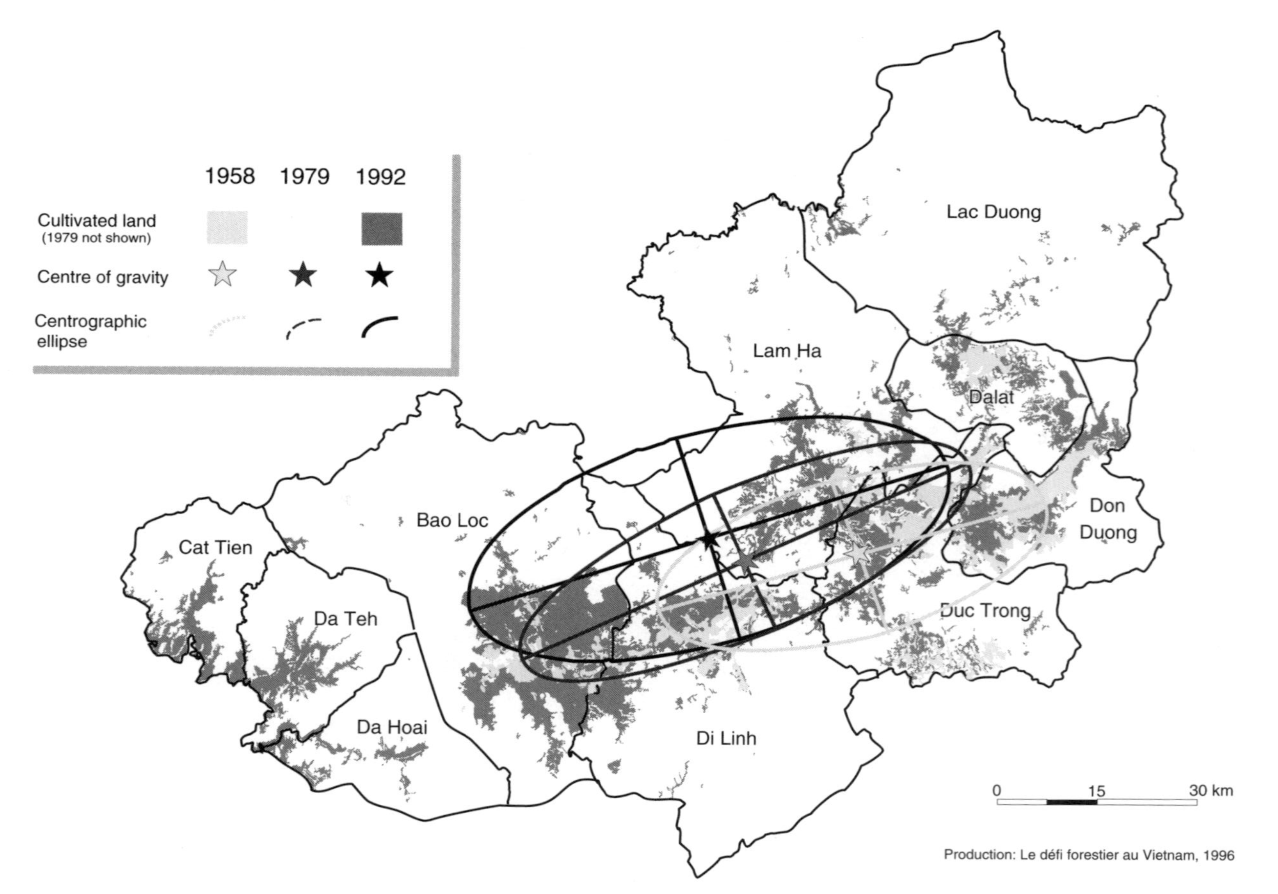

Figure 26. Lam Dong: spatiotemporal changes in cultivated land, 1958–92. Source: Subdivision No. 2, Forest Inventory and Planning Institute, Hanoi (1994 centrographic analysis).

timber market — it is very difficult to accurately account for all of its features. In any case, among the more evident illustrations of the dynamism of this progression, one provides a nearly indelible, if partial, testimony: the toponymic imprint.

Following a series of surveys concerning the origin of place names, which we reported elsewhere (De Koninck et al. 1996), we were able to reach a certain number of conclusions. One is that the toponymic imprint of the Kinh penetration in Lam Dong province is clearly evident in Cat Tien, Da Teh, and Lam Ha districts. In each of these, several communes bear names identical to those of Tonkinese or Annamese provinces (Figure 27). These are in fact the very districts that have received the majority of the more recent Kinh migrations (Tran Si Thu 1993). Overall, Tonkinese place names are very frequent on the frontier, which tends to confirm, if need be, that the Red River delta is a major reservoir for the colonists headed toward the Central Highlands.

In any case, the nature and specific local impact of Kinh pioneer settlements on the preestablished communities and on the environment have not been assessed to any great extent. In the context of our project, one study was recently completed in Don Duong district. Its specific purpose was to measure the degree of reliance on firewood among the communities of each of the nine communes making up that district, located in eastern Lam Dong. Among its findings were, first, further evidence of the pioneer communities' very high degree of dependency on the energy resources of the forest (for both domestic and cottage-industry purposes); and, second, the likelihood, unless consumption patterns are modified or new affordable resources are made available, that by 2004 the forest would no longer be able to meet the local demand without being itself irrevocably threatened. One of the other studies that emanated from our project and is currently under way aims to compare the overall living conditions prevailing among some pioneer settlements with those of the villages of the colonists' origin.

Other factors?

Even less than in Tuyen Quang province did the data made available to us and those we collected ourselves in Lam Dong allow us to specifically calculate the impact on the forest cover of the agricultural or other activities and practices of the ethnic minorities. Most likely, this impact is not negligible, not even in the district of Lac Duong, where Kinh settlers are still few and population density remains low. Furthermore, it remains to be verified whether this impact has been predominantly self-generated or results from external pressures exerted on the communities, notably by the expanding frontier. But whatever the nature and extent of that impact on the forest, it obviously cannot be compared with that of

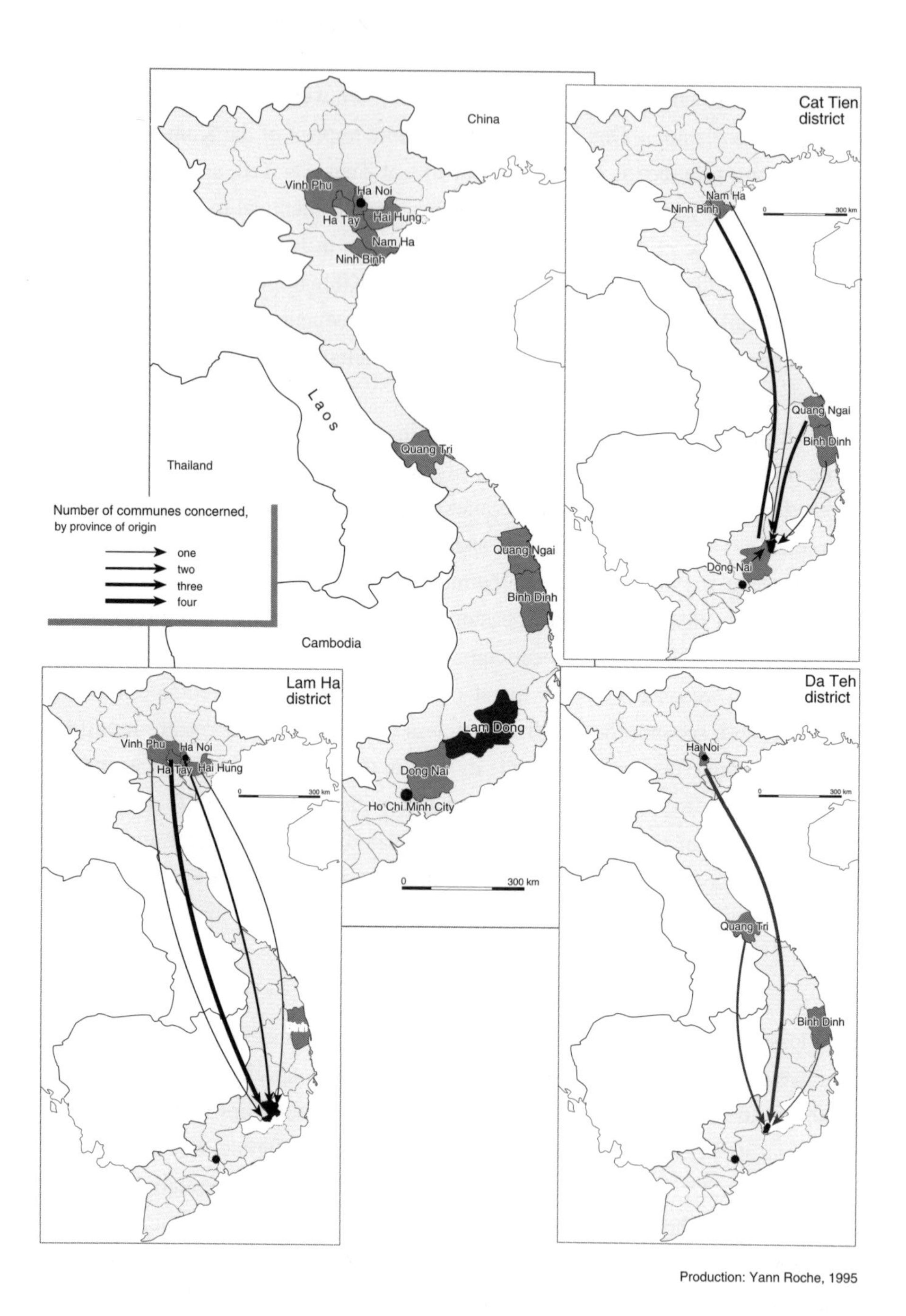

Figure 27. Lam Dong: origin of some commune names, 1994. Source: De Koninck et al. (1996); Tran Dac Dan, University of Agriculture and Forestry, Ho Chi Minh City (personal communication, 1996).

Kinh agricultural expansion, as illustrated by the comparison of land use in 1958, 1979, and 1992 (see Figures 19–21). This expansion, essentially a phenomenal enlargement of the areas devoted to the cultivation of cash crops, especially coffee, was possibly carried out, for a while, predominantly in areas blessed with basaltic soils. But this comparative advantage can no longer be evoked to explain the attraction of Lam Dong province, for it seems that for several decades now neither agricultural expansion nor land abandonment has taken place in areas that can be singled out pedologically. In other words, neither of these two processes has favoured or spared any specific type of soil (see Figures 17 and 19–21).

To anyone traveling through the Central Highlands, timber trade, including illegal timber trade, appears quite prevalent. In addition, it seems closely linked to agricultural expansion, with the cutting down and the clearing of large expanses of forests for cultivation generating huge quantities of a valuable commodity: timber. If the responsibility for the actual felling seems to lie mostly in the hands of the colonists themselves, the trading techniques and networks are not so easy to identify. In addition, the nibbling at the remaining surrounding forests, for which the settlers also seem to be responsible, may involve more than mere firewood or edible-plant collection — it may involve outright timber felling, including felling of large dipterocarpaceous trees. Evidently, such activities are not easily measured; nor is their specific impact. One thing is certain: they are largely linked to the dynamics of the frontier, in the midst of which numerous forms of trading and barter can prosper. The complexity of these marginal or clandestine activities and especially of the networks that link them is particularly great, given that their hinterland extends beyond the western borders of Viet Nam and that they occasionally involve representatives of the state. Obviously, much work lies ahead for the local and national authorities before order can be established on the frontier.

Finally, we attempted to find an answer to one last question: What were the short-, medium-, and long-term impacts of the defoliants sprayed on the forest by the US Air Force during the Viet Nam war? As it turned out, we were able, thanks to data provided by the FIPI, to construct a map schematically representing the distribution of sprayings that occurred over Lam Dong between 1968 and 1972; the western portion of the province, now corresponding to Cat Tien, Da Hoai, and Da Teh districts, was most affected. Juxtaposing this map next to the land-use maps for 1958 and 1979 (see Figures 19 and 20) is not very conclusive, to say the least. Notwithstanding the fact that traces of these sprayings are still evident on the ground near several villages, for example, in Cat Tien district, the actual land-use maps do not point to any meaningful correlation between the areas that had been sprayed with defoliants in 1968–72 and those that were without

forest cover in 1979. In Lam Dong, the reconstitution of forest cover in the defoliated areas does not seem to have been especially impaired. On other equally if not even more important issues, such as the long-term effect on soils and plants that may still have some harmful toxic content, we cannot provide any rigorous information, let alone any interpretation.

Chapter 6

CONCLUSION: THE MAGNITUDE OF THE CHALLENGE

Lacunae and findings

The Forest Challenge in Viet Nam project pursued two distinct yet complementary objectives: training and scientific analysis. Both were partially attained. Thus, at least 10 of the Vietnamese researchers involved in the project gained a lot of training. The same can be said of the slightly less numerous Canadian MA and PhD students who worked with the Vietnamese throughout the various phases of the 2-year project. The training dealt with research methods and techniques, as well as with research methodology, although most of the people involved, whether Vietnamese or Canadian, will admit that they also learned a lot about Viet Nam itself. The training would have been more intensive and elaborate had we been able to better handle communication problems, in all the meanings of the word *communication*, and to invest more in the project, mentally and in terms of time. Every member of the research team had several other pressing commitments, including and perhaps most of all the Vietnamese participants.

Among the scientific results of the project, a certain number of lacunae — but also some genuine findings or progress — can be identified. The causes and circumstances behind the lacunae have been dealt with at length in the first chapters. The actual nature of these lacunae essentially centres on our incapacity to truly measure and account for all the presumed causes of deforestation. More precisely, the problem was that we were unable to carry out a thorough diachronic analysis of all the factors initially and hypothetically identified as instrumental. Nevertheless, we did manage to decipher a few of them and, more importantly, to both demonstrate the validity of our central hypothesis and seriously question a number of so-called truths concerning the causes of deforestation in Viet Nam:

1. We were able to isolate several processes in time and space and to represent them cartographically, allowing us to point to Kinh agricultural expansion as the one major instrumental cause of deforestation. This was shown to be equally true for both Tuyen Quang and Lam Dong provinces.

2. Obviously, for the two provinces, the actual deforestation processes have followed somewhat different timetables. In Tuyen Quang province, located north of the Red River delta, deforestation, although still under way, was most intensive in the 1960s and 1970s. At that time, for war-related reasons, several of the provinces surrounding the delta had to host large numbers of migrants. Since the early 1980s, however, it seems that commercial concerns associated with the gigantic Bai Bang pulp and paper mill have become the major agents of deforestation. In contrast, in the Central Highlands province of Lam Dong, the retreat of the forest is closely associated with the ever-vigourous migration and agricultural expansion of the Kinh colonists, whether or not this modern form of agricultural expansion is officially backed by the Vietnamese state.

3. Tuyen Quang still appears much more deprived of its forests: the forests cling to only 7% of the provincial domain (in 1992), compared to 35% for their counterparts in Lam Dong. At least equally meaningful is the fact that barren lands dominate the Tuyen Quang landscape (64% of the land), a bad example, if not a bad omen, for the southern province — where such barren lands still account for "only" 20% of land use — if the advance of its frontier maintains its current pace.

4. We could even formulate the hypothesis of an historical commonality, an historical link between the different locations of the processes of deforestation. These processes would constitute one of the geographical repercussions of the advance of Kinh settlement. For several reasons, these repercussions, which were initially felt in the mountainous forested areas surrounding the Red River delta, have now reached the forested Central Highlands. This link even involves, as we have seen, members of ethnic communities: the Hmong and Nung people become, on behalf of Kinh colonists, territorial spearheads for the clearing of vast expanses of forest land, which are then devoted to the cultivation of cash crops.

5. It seems obvious, however, that even if some evidence suggests that a few members of ethnic minorities are involved in forms of agriculture that may lead to deforestation, the consequences are in no way comparable to those of the agricultural practices of Kinh colonists. In broad terms, it can be estimated that for each hectare of forest destroyed by the agricultural practices of the minorities, at least 20 ha is destroyed by those of the Kinh pioneers.

6. To this must be added an instrumental factor that becomes exceptionally active and significant in the context of pioneering agricultural expansion: wood and firewood collection by the new settlers. This gathering is particularly intensive, as the pioneers and settlers are often caught in situations of energy deficit, and in such situations wood and other forest products (including many that can be collected without forest clearing per se) become essential means of survival. Wood is also often used, legally or illegally, as house-construction material, but more importantly it is used as fuel for cooking food, including food for the pigs that many settlers raise (Brassard 1997).

7. Our study also allowed us to look more closely at geopolitical issues, especially whether agricultural expansion plays a geopolitical role in the integration of marginal and peripheral areas largely or even predominantly inhabited by ethnic minorities. The future of these minority groups remains closely linked to that of all the highlands of Viet Nam and therefore to the forest-protection and development policies implemented by the national Vietnamese authorities.

8. As pointed out by Rambo (1995), the policies that relate to planning for and managing the development of the uplands solely in the interests of the dominant ethnic community are not specific to Viet Nam. In this country, just as in several others in Southeast Asia, such policies were consolidated during the colonial period. In Viet Nam, the consequences have been particularly disastrous for the ethnic minorities, whose overall living conditions appear very precarious indeed.

The future of minority peoples, as well as that of the forest domain that most of these peoples inhabit or at least use, depends not only on specific national policies but also on cooperation among nations in the region. For example, the environmental and commercial policies of Thailand — whose industrial sector has been growing very rapidly over the last three decades and which has severely curtailed, if not banned, all forms of logging — have a direct impact on the fate of the forest in the three neighbouring countries of Cambodia, Laos, and Myanmar. In these neighbouring countries, numerous agents, ranging from multinational companies to small smugglers, try, legally or illegally, to satisfy the resulting greater demand for wood and for hydroelectric energy. Even agricultural-expansion policies, particularly of the kind involving cash crops, are largely conditioned by the world market. This broadens the stakes in a context where the policies of international organizations, particularly the World Bank and the International Monetary Fund (IMF), bear a large responsibility.

In Southeast Asia, it is conceivable that the panregional consolidation of the Association of Southeast Asian Nations will allow its nine members to better consult each other regarding their social and environmental policies, with the understanding that the two types of policy remain closely linked and should condition their political and economic policies, not the other way around.

Thus, the management of the forest heritage is an issue that must be dealt with at all geographical scales — whether local, national, panregional, or even global. For example, since mid-1997, massive operations using fire to clear land for agricultural expansion in Indonesia have had severe and detrimental environmental consequences throughout much of the rest of Southeast Asia. Although the Indonesian authorities did recognize publicly and for the first time that ethnic minorities were not to blame, but rather that agricultural expansion (basically for oil palm) was the main culprit, very little has been done to curb the dangerous practice. The world-market demand is still there for palm oil, rubber, plywood, etc. So, given the current predicament of the Indonesian economy, the World Bank and the IMF are likely to continue to support all forms of export policies, even those whose social and environmental consequences are clearly questionable.

In such a context, it is crucial that researchers remain active on all fronts, documenting, analyzing, and interpreting what is really happening at the ground level, where people live.

What to do?

It is quite evident that the limited scope and modest scientific results of the research project do not allow us to draw a definitive conclusion, in absolute and peremptory terms, about all the causes of deforestation in Viet Nam and even less about all the policies required to bring it under control. However, as we have made some headway in identifying some of the main instrumental causes of the retreat of the forest and the articulations that link them operationally, I feel entitled to make some recommendations.

Before I get into these, it seems appropriate to recall that, as stated in the introductory chapter, Viet Nam is already one of the least-forested countries in the region, if not the least forested. Obviously, time is of the essence; the forest continues to retreat rapidly, probably more rapidly than most observers will admit. As already discussed, in the province of Lam Dong alone, more than 10 000 ha of forest is cleared annually: this corresponds to about 2% of the remaining provincial forest cover. But the three other still heavily forested provinces of the Central

Highlands (Dac Lac, Gia Lai, and Kon Tum) are also being taken to task — especially Dac Lac — and probably at an even heavier pace. Overall, as stated earlier, it can be estimated that the forests of Viet Nam recede by more than 200 000 ha/year. Estimates of the proportion of the country still forested in 1997 vary between 10 and 20%, that is, between some 3.3 million and 6.6 million ha. In other words, the national annual rate of deforestation stands between 3 and 6%.

1. If the Vietnamese government does have the will to cope with the forest challenge, that is, the will to implement policies to support the optimal use, protection, and rehabilitation of the dwindling forest heritage, it is imperative that the government reexamine its own policies of commercial forest exploitation and, even more, those of agricultural expansion.

2. After the research report (on which this book is based) was handed in to IDRC at the very end of 1996, Vietnamese authorities in fact began to proclaim drastic measures designed to better protect the country's forests. Thus, in April and May 1997, the Ministry of Agriculture and Rural Development decreed that all natural forests would be closed to commercial logging, at the same time forbidding all forms of spontaneous migrations into forest areas (*Viet Nam News*, 8 June 1997). But the government's spokesperson made no mention of state-sponsored agricultural expansion. On the contrary, this seems to be vigorously encouraged, as new areas are being opened — primarily in the Central Plateaus but also in Dong Nai province (Roussel and Hoang 1997) and even in some coastal provinces — for cultivation of export crops. Among these coffee and rubber predominate. In fact, both of these crops are the object of extremely ambitious programs, which in the case of rubber includes a planned expansion from some 290 000 ha in 1996 to 750 000 ha by 2005 (Eschbach and Tran 1997).

3. Given the obvious persistence and magnitude of the agricultural-expansion policies, as well as the already heavy impact of the NEZs (demonstrated above and emphasized by authors such as Sikor [1995]), it seems essential that the Vietnamese authorities and their various partners permit and facilitate permanent monitoring of the environmental impacts of this expansion on the few remaining stands of natural forests. These include the so-called downstream impacts — those felt in the lowlands, whose environmental health (water, soil, energy, etc.) depends so much on the natural equilibrium of the highlands.

4. The scientific and social objectives of these studies should be clearly and specifically defined, and their pursuit should rely on attempts to verify a series of hypotheses through appropriate methods and means.

5. These investigations should deal with a whole set of objects and propositions related to the problem of the optimal use of the dwindling natural forests. The results may point to a need to broaden and improve current forest-protection and -rehabilitation policies and, more fundamentally, their implementation.

Researchers should undertake interrelated analyses of specific objects, including the following.

Indigenous knowledge and use of biodiversity

An assessment of the Vietnamese forests' biodiversity was among the initial objectives of our research project. Unfortunately, for reasons explained earlier, this assessment has remained embryonic. It now seems more realistic and preferable to undertake new, less ambitious, and more localized research. The object of study could be a relatively restricted forest domain, well defined and known to be threatened, for example, a small river valley or a watershed of modest dimensions, possibly in Lam Dong or even in Tuyen Quang. Special consideration should be given to the local population's knowledge and use of forest resources and biodiversity. The study should in fact involve both a community of Kinh colonists and an ethnic-minority community. After all, if biodiversity is to be properly assessed and protected, what better research agents can be found than the very people who rely for their daily survival on an intimate knowledge of the forest resources?

New settlers' nibbling

A study should be carried out of the gradual degradation of a given forest area attributed to a community of Kinh colonists. This degradation might result from the nibbling at the forest bordering a recent settlement as the pioneers collect, on an almost daily basis, firewood and various types of wood, bamboo, and rattan for construction, along with edible and medicinal plants. This degradation may also be accelerated by the opening of swidden fields that eventually become permanently cultivated or are abandoned because of lack of fertility or massive soil deterioration and erosion. Ideally, the study should be undertaken in the same area as the analysis of biodiversity mentioned above.

Ethnic minorities' nibbling

A study of ethnic minorities' nibbling at the forest should be designed and carried out to allow a comparison with the results of the study of the influence of Kinh colonists. The two studies could be done concurrently in a restricted and well-defined area. The definition of the area might need to be dynamic if the chosen minority community practices some form or other of nomadic swidden agriculture.

Energy requirements

As a complement to the two previously mentioned studies of forest degradation, a more focused study might deal with the specific issue of energy requirements, sources, and uses by a community of colonists, as well as by an ethnic-minority community. The choice of the respondent communities should of course be articulated with those of the previous studies.

Commercial exploitation

Few of the many existing forms of commercial exploitation of the ligneous resources of the forest are easy to investigate. But in Viet Nam one venture, although complex, definitely deserves to be the object of a thorough analysis. I am thinking of the Bai Bang pulp and paper mill, the largest in the country. An in-depth study of its history and of its geography, that is, of the hinterland that provides not only its raw-material supply but also its labour supply, would be bound to yield a wealth of information related to the forest challenge.

Forest protection

Among forest-related issues is, of course, the need to somehow protect the forest domain, or at least part of it. Besides the various laws designed to protect, or at least to ensure a proper use of, forest areas, some aim to ensure their total, "definitive" protection through the establishment of national forest parks. A national forest park might be the object of a systematic analysis taking into account not only what it is protected for, in principle, but also the actual results. Here again the choice of the study site (for example, in Cat Tien district) should be articulated as much as possible with that of the other investigations.

Reforestation

The idea of forest protection inevitably evokes the idea of reforestation. Reforestation and replanting policies are numerous and complex. This should not prevent researchers from attempting to look closely at a specific reforestation program through a case study of a well-defined area where replanting has been active and where it is possible to evaluate survival rates, environmental impacts, and the involvement of local populations. The study would be that much more fruitful if carried out in the same regions as all the above-mentioned investigations.

Agricultural expansion

Overall, it does seem almost superfluous to study Vietnamese forests if (as we found) the fundamental agent of their destruction, namely, agricultural-expansion policies, is not questioned and scrutinized. In other words, my first recommendation is that all the fundamentals and implications of these policies should be put at the top of any research agenda concerning the forest challenge in Viet Nam.

To actually implement this agenda, a multidisciplinary approach and well-articulated case studies are needed. In turn, for such articulations to be meaningful and for their scientific results to be useful to policymakers, near-permanent methodological concertations among the researchers are needed. In this manner, the already positive results of The Forest Challenge in Viet Nam project, in terms of both training and analysis, are likely to be further enhanced. But this will be better achieved if Vietnamese scholars and planners produce their own rigorous, field-based analyses and interpretations of this challenge and all its ramifications and implications. Given the already ongoing follow-up to the above project, that seems like a realistic proposition.

Appendix 1

ACRONYMS AND ABBREVIATIONS

asl	above sea level
CRES	Center for Natural Resources and Environmental Studies
FIPI	Forest Inventory and Planning Institute
HCMC	Ho Chi Minh City
IDRC	International Development Research Centre
IMF	International Monetary Fund
NCSS	National Centre for the Social Sciences
NEZ	New Economic Zone
UAF	University of Agriculture and Forestry

REFERENCES

Bairoch, P. 1995. Mythes et paradoxes de l'histoire économique mondiale. La Découverte, Paris, France. 286 pp.

Bernard, S.; De Koninck, R. 1996. The retreat of the forest in Southeast Asia: a cartographic assessment. Singapore Journal of Tropical Geography, 17(1), 1–14.

Boulbet, J. 1975. Les paysans de la forêt. École française d'Extrême-Orient, Paris, France. 146 pp.

——— 1995. Vers un sens de la terre / Towards a sense of the Earth. Prince of Songkla University, Hat Yai, Songkla, Thailand. 138 pp.

Brassard, F. 1997. Le bois-énergie parmi les communautés des Hautes-Terres du Vietnam. Faculté de foresterie et de géomatique, Laval University, Québec, PQ, Canada. MA thesis. 149 pp.

Brocheux, P.; Hémery, D. 1994. Indochine : la colonisation ambiguë. La Découverte, Paris, France. 427 pp.

Buchy, M. 1993. Histoire forestière de l'Indochine (1850–1954) : perspectives de recherche. Revue française d'histoire d'Outre-Mer, 80(299), 219–249.

Colchester, M. 1993. Colonizing the rainforests: the agents and causes of deforestation. *In* Colchester, M.; Lohman, L., ed., The struggle for land and the fate of the forest. Zed Books, London, UK. pp. 1–15.

Collins, M., ed. 1990. The last rain forests. a world conservation atlas. Oxford University Press, New York, NY. 200 pp.

Collins, M.; Sayer, J.; Whitmore, T. 1991. The conservation atlas of tropical forests: Asia and the Pacific. Simon and Schuster, Toronto, ON, Canada. 256 pp.

Condominas, G. 1957. Nous avons mangé la forêt de la Pierre Génie-Gôo. Mercure de France, Paris, France. 433 pp.

Conklin, H.C. 1961. The study of shifting cultivation. Current Anthropology, 2, 27–61.

De Koninck, R. 1986. La paysannerie comme fer de lance territorial de l'État : le cas de la Malaysia. Cahiers des sciences humaines (ORSTOM), 22(3–4), 355–370.

——— 1993. Le compromis territorial. Cahiers des sciences humaines (ORSTOM), 30th anniversary edition, 43–47.

——— 1994. L'Asie du Sud-Est. Masson, Paris, France. 317 pp.

——— 1996. The peasantry as the territorial spearhead of the state: the case of Vietnam. Sojourn: Social Isssues in Southeast Asia, 11(2), 231–258.

——— 1998. La logique de la déforestation en Asie du Sud-Est. Cahiers d'Outre-Mer, 201. (In press.)

De Koninck, R.; Déry, S. 1997. Agricultural expansion as a tool of population redistribution in Southeast Asia. Journal of Southeast Asian Studies, 28(1), 1–26.

De Koninck, R.; Tran Dac Dan; Roche, Y.; Lundqvist, O. 1996. Les fronts pionniers du centre du Viêt-nam : évolution démographique et empreinte toponymique. Annales de géographie, 590, 395–412.

Do Dinh Sam. 1994. Shifting cultivation in Vietnam: its social, economic and environmental values relative to alternative land use. International Institute for Environment and Development, London, UK. 56 pp.

Dove, M. 1983. Theories of swidden agriculture and the political economy of ignorance. Agroforestry Systems, 1, 85–99.

Eschbach, J.-M.; Tran Thi Thuy Hoa. 1997. L'hévéaculture au Vietnam : projet de développement de la région du centre. Agriculture et développement, 15, 199–208.

ESRI (Environmental Systems Research Institute, Inc.). 1992. Digital map of the world. Developed for the US Defense Mapping Agency. ESRI, Redlands, CA, USA.

Gourou, P. 1940. L'utilisation du sol en Indochine française. Publications du Centre d'études de politique étrangère, Paris, France. 466 pp.

——— 1947a. Les pays tropicaux. Les presses universitaires de France, Paris, France. 197 pp.

——— 1947b. La terre et l'homme en Extrême-Orient. Armand Colin, Paris, France. 224 pp.

——— 1953. The tropical world. Longmans, London, UK. [Translation of *Les pays tropicaux*, 1947.] 196 pp.

Gourou, P.; Loubet, J. 1934. Géographie de l'Indochine. Imprimerie Tonkinoise, Hanoi, Viet Nam. 160 pp.

Haudricourt, A.G. 1974. Le nom du champ sur brûlis et le nom de la rizière. Études rurales, 53–56, 467–472.

Hickey, G.C. 1982a. Sons of the mountains: ethnohistory of the Vietnamese Central Highlands to 1954. Yale University Press, New Haven, CT, USA. 488 pp.

——— 1982b, Free in the forest: ethnohistory of the Vietnamese Central Highlands 1954–1976. Yale University Press, New Haven, CT, USA. 350 pp.

Hill, R. 1985. "Primitives" to peasants? The "sedentarisation" of the nomads of Vietnam. Pacific Viewpoint, 26(2), 449–457.

IGA (Instituto Geographico de Agostini). 1969. World atlas of agriculture. IGA, Novara, Italy. 146 pp.

Lang, C. 1997. Bai Bang pulp and paper mill: paper tiger? Watershed, 2(3), 35–38.

LDPSB (Lam Dong Provincial Statistics Bureau). 1981. Sô liêu thông kê tinh Lâm Dông 1976–1980. LDPSB, Dalat, Viet Nam. 262 pp.

Lebar, F.M.; Hickey, G.C.; Musgrave, J.K. 1964. Ethnic groups of mainland Southeast Asia. Human Relations Area Files Press, New Haven, CT, USA. 288 pp.

Le Thac Can; Vo Quy. 1994. Vietnam: environmental issues and possible solutions. Asian Journal of Environmental Management, 2(2), 69–77.

Maurand, P. 1943. L'Indochine forestière. Imprimerie d'Extrême-Orient, Hanoi, Viet Nam. 121 pp.

——— 1968. Politique forestière à envisager au Vietnam dans l'après-guerre. Institut de recherches agronomiques, Ministère des réformes agraires et de l'agriculture, Saigon, Viet Nam. 60 pp.

MOF (Ministry of Forestry). 1991. Vietnam forestry sector review. Tropical Forestry Action Programme: main report. Ministry of Forestry, Hanoi, Viet Nam.

Morgan, J.R.; Valencia, M.J. 1983. Atlas for marine policy in Southeast Asian seas. University of California Press, Berkeley, CA, USA. 146 pp.

Nguyen Van Thang. 1995. The Hmong and Dzao people in Vietnam: impact of traditional socioeconomic and cultural factors on the protection and development of forest resources. *In* Rambo, T.; Reed, R.R.; Le Trong Cuc; DiGregorio, M.R., ed., The challenges of highland development in Vietnam. East–West Center, Program on Environment, Honolulu, HI, USA; University of Hanoi, Center for Natural Resources and Environmental Studies, Hanoi, Viet Nam; University of California, Center for Southeast Asian Studies, Berkeley, CA, USA. pp. 101–119.

Pouchepadass, J. 1993. Colonisations et environnement. Revue française d'histoire d'outre-mer, 72 (268): 5-22.

Rambo, A.T. 1995. Defining highland development challenges in Vietnam. *In* Rambo, T.; Reed, R.R.; Le Trong Cuc; DiGregorio, M.R., ed., The challenges of highland development in Vietnam. East–West Center, Program on Environment, Honolulu, HI, USA; University of Hanoi, Center for Natural Resources and Environmental Studies, Hanoi, Viet Nam; University of California, Center for Southeast Asian Studies, Berkeley, CA, USA. pp. xi–xxvii.

Roussel, A.; Hoang Huu Cai. 1997. Expansion et développement agricoles : le cas de la province de Dong Nai. Agriculture et développement, 15, 145–154.

Sargent, C. 1991. Forestry sector review: Tropical Forestry Action Plan. Vietnam: land use issues. Ministry of Forestry, Hanoi, Viet Nam; United Nations Development Programme, New York, NY, USA; Food and Agriculture Organization of the United Nations, Rome, Italy. 36 pp.

Sikor, T. 1995. Decree 327 and the restoration of barren land in the Vietnamese highlands. *In* Rambo, T.; Reed, R.R.; Le Trong Cuc; DiGregorio, M.R., ed., The challenges of highland development in Vietnam. East–West Center, Program on Environment, Honolulu, HI, USA; University of Hanoi, Center for Natural Resources and Environmental Studies, Hanoi, Viet Nam; University of California, Center for Southeast Asian Studies, Berkeley, CA, USA. pp. 143–156.

Spencer, J.E. 1966. Shifting cultivation in southeastern Asia. University of California Press, Berkeley and Los Angeles, CA, USA. 247 pp.

Thrupp, L.A.; Hecht, S.B.; Browder, J.O.; et al. 1997. The diversity and dynamics of shifting cultivation: myths, realities and policy implications. World Resources Institute, Washington, DC, USA. 48 pp.

Tran Si Thu. 1992. Some problems about Lam Dong population. Bureau of Statistics, Dalat, Viet Nam. 78 pp.

——— 1993. Lam Dong–Dalat: a promising region for investment. Department of Culture Information, Dalat, Viet Nam.

Tran Thi Van An; Nguyen Manh Huan. 1995. Changing rural institutions and social relations. *In* Kerkvliet, B.J.T.; Porter, D.J., ed., Vietnam's rural transformation. Westview Press, Boulder, CO, USA. pp. 201–214.

Vo Quy. 1996. The environmental challenges of Vietnam's development. *In* Draft report. Regional Seminar on Environmental Education, 19–22 March 1996, University of Hanoi, Center for Natural Resources and Environmental Studies, Hanoi, Viet Nam. pp. 4–20.

Vo Quy; Le Thac Can. 1994. Conservation of forest resources and the greater biodiversity of Vietnam. Asian Journal of Environmental Management, 2(2), 55–59.

Weisberg, B. 1970. Ecocide in Indochina: the ecology of war. Canfield Press, San Fransisco, CA, USA.

Weltforstat Atlas. 1971. Weltforstat atlas. Paul Parey, Hamburg, Germany. 272 pp.

Whitmore, T.C. 1984. Tropical rain forests of the Far East (2nd ed.). Clarendon, Oxford, UK. 352 pp.

——— 1990. An introduction to tropical rain forests. Oxford University Press, New York, NY, USA. 226 pp.

WCMC (World Conservation Monitoring Centre). 1996. The Socialist Republic of Vietnam. Internet: http://www.wcmc.org.uk/infoserv/countryp/vietnam/index.htm

The Institution

The International Development Research Centre (IDRC) is committed to building a sustainable and equitable world. IDRC funds developing-world researchers, thus enabling the people of the South to find their own solutions to their own problems. IDRC also maintains information networks and forges linkages that allow Canadians and their developing-world partners to benefit equally from a global sharing of knowledge. Through its actions, IDRC is helping others to help themselves.

The Publisher

IDRC Books publishes research results and scholarly studies on global and regional issues related to sustainable and equitable development. As a specialist in development literature, IDRC Books contributes to the body of knowledge on these issues to further the cause of global understanding and equity. IDRC publications are sold through its head office in Ottawa, Canada, as well as by IDRC's agents and distributors around the world.

The Author

Rodolphe De Koninck is Professor of Geography at Université Laval in Ste-Foy (Canada). His research experience in Asia is extensive. Prof. De Koninck received his doctorate in geography from the University of Singapore in 1970 and, among his many visiting professorships, are stints at Shanghai International University and the National University of Singapore. His research has focused on Indonesia, Malaysia, Singapore, the Philippines, China, Bangladesh, and Viet Nam. He is the author of *Le monde à la carte* (Fischer Presses, 1990), *L'Asie de Sud-Est* (Masson, 1994), and editor of *The Challenge of the Forest in Southeast Asia* (GÉRAC, 1994), as well as many other books and research papers. Prof. De Koninck is a member of the Royal Society of Canada and currently President of the Canadian Council for Southeast Asian Studies. He was recently awarded the 1998 Prix Jacques-Rousseau for interdisciplinarity by the Association canadienne-française pour l'avancement des sciences (Acfas).

Lvm 655 8847 250 Bevin #407